HOME IS a dirty STREET

HOME IS A DIRTY STREET

THE SOCIAL OPPRESSION OF BLACK CHILDREN

by Eugene Perkins

Third World Press   **Chicago**

This book is dedicated to the memory of James Johnson, Michael Robinson, Michael Soto, John Soto, Steven McClinton and other black youths whose lives have been shortened by the politics of capitalism, racism and colonialism.

INTRODUCTION

To simply offer a noteworthy appraisal of Eugene Perkins' book is to participate in a rhetorical exercise which we, as a Black and un-empowered community, have had too much of and could well do without.

For praise, plaudits and platitudes were not the factors that motivated this Black author and social agent to present this social treatise for our consideration and our concern.

Indeed, it is more accurate to state that Perkins, the man is more involved with another and far more fundamental issue in this social commentary: that Blacks should begin to chronicle—assess, appraise, evaluate and predict—their own lifestyle and the conditions that contribute to whatever we are or hope to be.

Perkins presents Lawndale, then, as merely a microcosm of any and all other areas we live in as an excluded people. Speaking thus in *Home Is A Dirty Street,* Perkins delivers the message of *need* from several vantage points: gut-felt need for survival which are economically rooted; need for self-worth, self-esteem and self-expression which are culturally rooted; and need for redemption and re-direction on the part of Blacks who purport to serve but whose allegiances are all-too-often pledged to everyone except Blacks which are politically rooted.

It is essential then to our experience as Blacks that we give undivided attention to the fact that Perkins presents for us a glimpse into Lawndale—not with himself directly involved (except as part of his life work) but with the unspoken but urgent appeal for the involvement of us all. His grace and style of understatement, his apparent flailing of person and energy that borders at times upon understandable instances of near-hoplessness, his tendency to restrain from the "beating of the drum" which has already called too many to falsely represent our cause—must not be mistaken nor overlooked in these strivings of a man such as Perkins who has genuinely and unremittingly pledged his life to services that go far beyond the limits of this work.

Therefore, in order to properly introduce *Home Is A Dirty Street* it is also proper to state a few simple but honest things about Eugene Perkins, the man. Modest and almost always personally embarrassed to a flaw, Eugene (or, better, "Gene", as we all call him) does not simply have a *JOB* in a social service agency in Lawndale. He *WORKS* in Lawndale, as in all other arenas of his concern, which is fundamentally different. There is no splitting or splintering of his psyche which causes him to "hat up" at closing hours and rejoin to other quarters where he assesses, interprets and evaluates "those people" in the same manner of white social agents (and sociologists) and, again, all-too-many Black brothers and sisters who have *jobs* among "them" but no longer consider themselves an intricate part *of* "them".

As a social agency employee, Gene never sees himself removed from what occurs in Lawndale and other similarly constrained Black communities throughout this nation. He will not only assist in the establishment of recreation centers and programs, but he is always actively involved in the life equations that propel a child or youth—or his parents and other adults—to adhere more to the world and the phenomena of the streets with all the social consequences. And when these consequences lead to incidents that hurl Black youths and Black people against the walls of what Gene newly terms as a "Ghetcolony", he is equally as attendent to their needs and responses as supervised offenders, paroled offenders and long-termed and short-termed inmates in various penal institutions.

Gene Perkins serves Black youths in particular and Black people in general from the internalized conviction of himself—as a Black man *first,* and then as an organizer, writer, poet, husband, father and friend. He denotes and reflects the rhythm of countless others who view themselves as those who spring from the womb of a Culture to which they are inextricably linked and committed in terms of its well-being, its survival and its extension into all futures.

Home Is A Dirty Street, then, cannot be fully appreciated except in the first full recognition of the presenter. Gene's turning from praise and adulation created sufficient problems, even with his acceptance of this introduction. These qualities should, however, shed better light on two important factors that are direly needed in our surge for total liberation; namely, re-definition of leaders and leadership and re-alignment of our values that will cause us to hold more accountable all who purport to lead.

Against this background, Blacks—the sole audience of Perkins' work—must discern and internalize the realities of life in a machine-controlled Chicago. We must understand Lawndale as but part of the overall spectre which hovers over us and haunts us from every conceivable and salient point of our lives. For when human beings of a culture are so hopelessly trapped in any one segment of their total experience, there is and cannot be anything other than paltry semblances or illusions of escape or empowerment for all other segments of that culture.

We must deal openly and honestly with all of the Lawndales of our lives and better cast our understandings, our experiences and our energies in the light of not only local urgencies, but national and international urgencies as well.

For, indeed, Blacks stand in more perilous circumstances than ever experienced in this country. As political, economic and other institutionalized entities of the dominant culture wrestle with problems that they themselves must resolve with better persuasion, the truth of new technologies and systems are that fewer people are considered in terms of the earth's population and the earth's resources. And where at one point in time Blacks had to be concerned about our mental and spiritual well-being, indeed, now, our actual physical presence in the universe is seriously threatened.

The annals of history and the pathways of the present have been littered with the debris of racial constraint. All Blacks have resided and continue to reside on one *dirty street* or another. It will be only through the patient and non-self-seeking strivings of men such as Gene Perkins that we must acquaint ourselves with more sustaining dwelling places.

Lu Palmer

TABLE OF CONTENTS

Foreword

This book is a reflection of my sixteen years of working with black ghetcolony children in Chicago. (The term ghetcolony is defined in Chapter One). As a youth worker, I have seen the lives of a countless number of black children destroyed by mis-education, substandard housing, police brutality, corrupt politics, deplorable sanitary conditions, inadequate health facilities, damaged self-concepts and institutional racism. *Home Is A Dirty Street* is not a study but a commentary which attempts to explain how the system of oppression prevents urban black children from achieving their true potentials. There are few institutions in the black ghetcolony structured to assist the black child to adequately cope with the overwhelming pressures imposed on him by the larger society. He is expected to be socially adjusted, morally sound and free of so-called anti-social behavior, yet his environment represents the antithesis of these virtues.

In the public schools the black child is indoctrinated with the pioneering romanticism of the "American Way of Life," but this society provides him with few opportunities to achieve this goal. Then there are the social service agencies which find refuge in the black ghetcolony to exalt their missionary image. And the religious institutions continue to chastise black children for being obnoxious delinquents. And black children are constantly being harrassed, intimidated and even killed by quick-tempered policemen who feel that the gun is the only way to deal with their sometimes volatile expressions. As a result of these oppressive forces, black children are forced to find their "supports" in the Street Institution, where they learn the coping skills needed to survive under a system of oppression. Their teachers are the men who have themselves grown up in the ghetcolony and often the street gang becomes their greatest ally. The "rights of passage" are constantly being denied them, for their life in the ghetcolony seldom allows them to become self-actualizing persons.

It has been these and other things which motivated me to write about how the system of oppression in America is destroying black children before our very eyes, with few people or institutions doing anything about it. This book is concerned with the social plight of the black ghetcolony child as it relates to his total development and his entry into the adult world.

Although there have been other books describing the world of black children, most of these have dealt with the case histories of rural black children and were written between the period of 1940-50. Some of the more notable ones have been: Allison Davis and John Dollar's *Children of Bondage,* Charles S. Johnson's *Growing Up In The Black Belt,* and E. Franklin Frazier's *Negro Youth At The Crossway.* In recent years we have been able to get another glimpse of black children growing up in the ghetcolony through contemporary novels like Claude Brown's *Manchild In The Promised Land,* Imamu Amiri Baraka's *The System Of Dante's Hell* and George Cain's *Blueschild Baby.* But these books too. though highly descriptive of life in the black ghetcolony, basically reflect case histories. There have also been a deluge of books, consisting of excerpts from novels or essays by individuals, which describe what it's like growing up in the black ghetcolony. However, these books tend to give only fragmented details and deal mainly with so-called successful blacks who have been able to rise above the ghetcolony.

Of course, many white social scientists continue to define the black child from their alienated perspective and while some of their studies are academically stimulating, they fail to present a clear analysis of the total social factors (capitalism, racism and colonialization) which oppress the black child. Instead, most of their studies only reinforce the traditional theories of pathological behavior which have been used to define the behavior of black children.

Although *Home Is A Dirty Street* draws heavily from my experiences with black children in North Lawndale, a black ghetcolony of Chicago, I feel that it also reflects the patterns of growing up in Harlem, Bedford Stuyvesant and other black communities. Like most books, it has its share of flaws, ambivalences and mistakes, all of which I assume full responsibility for. But it is a sincere effort, on my part, to share with others the reasons why black children become victimized and wards of a society which has no place for them.

I would like to extend appreciation to the Board of Directors of the Better Boys Foundation and its Executive Director, Warner S. Saunders, who were kind enough to allow me the time to write my manuscript. And to Joseph Hoffman for his encouragement. And Robert MacRae, Executive Director of the Chicago Community Trust, who helped me to get a small grant to begin my book. And I would like to give special thanks to Sister Maria Mootry and Sister Doris (Ajua) Barnett who edited the manuscript and to Sister Diane Glenn for her meticulous typing. Also, I would like to thank my publisher for allowing me the opportunity to express my ideas freely, Lerone Bennett, Senior Editor of *Ebony Magazine* and Lou Palmer, Editor of the *Black X-Press* for their support and criticism. And, of course, I give thanks to my beautiful wife, Janis, who allowed me to keep our small dining room table cluttered with books and papers without complaining once.

CHAPTER ONE

NORTH LAWNDALE:
ANATOMY OF A BLACK GHETCOLONY

Negroes in Bronzeville are very much Americans. And this means, too, that if the masses are driven too far they are likely to fight back, despite their sometimes seemingly indifferent reactions to discrimination and segregation. A potential for future violence within Black Metropolis exists that should not and cannot be ignored.

St. Clair Drake and
Horace R. Clayton

Black Metropolis

Growing up in North Lawndale is more than a challenge. It is a feat that defies the manner in which children are suppose to live in this society. The very fact that they manage to endure this oppressed community is an achievement which contradicts the great odds that are stacked against them. Although they are born into a society that claims to offer a higher standard of living than any other large nation, the benefits from this prosperity fails to touch their lives. Instead, these neglected and often misguided youths receive the barest of this country's vast resources, and are dependent upon their own survival skills to cope with the oppressive elements in their environment. And despite a constant plot to destroy them, somehow most manage to survive. However, the manner in which they survive should be viewed as a travesty of American justice.

North Lawndale is located on Chicago's far West Side, near the white suburb of Cicero, Illinois, where Jerome Huey, a fifteen year old black youth, was clubbed to death in 1965, and where the late Dr. Martin Luther King Jr.'s Freedom Movement of 1966 confronted the Zenith of northern white racism.

In many ways, North Lawndale is a typical urban black community. Like Bedford Stuyvesant in Brooklyn, Hough district in Cleveland, and the blighted streets of Harlem, it contains all of the social maladies which sociologists label as being underprivileged, culturally deprived, disadvantaged and from which a voluminous number of books have been written to describe what it is like to be poor and black in America. But few social experts ever depict the real reasons these communities have become deprived sanctuaries for the suppression of black children.

An honest analysis of these urban communities will reveal them to be the products of an oppressive system that has systematically relegated their inhabitants to a status not much higher than what black people endured during the days of legalized slavery. In fact, in many ways, the black urban community is only an extension of the old plantation system which so cruelly attempted to uproot the original culture of black people. This simply means that it still bears the scars of social, economic and political exploitation. But, of course, the deeply rooted hypocrisy in this country will not allow America to admit this fact. And in an effort to camouflage her wanton oppression of black people, white sociologists have conjectured all kinds of theories to explain why black people are disenfranchised members of this society. However, because the situation of black people in America has been so unique, these theories have never been able to adequately define its peculiar manifestations. Having been conceived from a White Anglo-Saxon

Protestant (WASP) frame of reference, these theories have no legitimate basis for defining the situation of black people. They have been skewed in such a manner that they either rationalize a justification for oppression or concoct studies to disprove its existence. Consequently, communities like North Lawndale are conveniently classified as "ghettos" because of the less oppressive connotation this word implies. When black people first began migrating to cities in large numbers, the word ghetto became synonymous with the communities where they were forced to live. Although this country has Jewish ghettos, Polish ghettos, Irish ghettos and other types of ghettos, the word ghetto takes on a special stigma when it is applied to the black community. It suggests a community that is maligned with crime, slums, deprivation and social disorganization. While these conditions do prevail, in varying proportions, in the black community, they tend to only reflect the aftermath of social deterioration rather than the system of oppression which breeds such conditions. As a result, black people are conditioned to coping with so-called "ghetto problems" instead of combating the system of oppression that perpetuates them. Black people are not oppressed because of the deteriorating elements in their community. They are oppressed because of a political system, disguised under the name of democracy, which has never felt them worthy enough to be free people. But the black urban community is more than a so-called ghetto and only by redefining its true character will black people begin to understand the oppressive system that creates it and the manifestations it embodies. Without these new definitions, black people will, most likely, continue to seek solutions which are not applicable to their unique situation in America.

In recent years, there have been some black people who feel that the word colony best describes the black community. While the black community does not have all of the characteristics common to a colony, its oppressive status clearly indicates that it is exploited by another group. Also, since black people were brought to this country as subjects of a foreign country, they were denied citizenship until the so-called Emancipation Proclamation. But black people have never gained full equality as American citizens, and, therefore, can still be considered subjects under foreign domination. And if the oppression of black people in America is to be fully revealed, it must be identified by political terms and not sociological jargon. In the following diagram, I have listed the dominant characteristics of the so-called ghetto and the colony. I have then extracted from each, those characteristics which are most typical of the systems that oppress the urban black community. After fusing these characteristics, I have, for the purpose of this book, arrived at a term which I choose to call the black ghetcolony.

GHETTO	COLONY
Relocated ethnic population	Indigenous ethnic population
Controlled by native government	Controlled by foreign government
Attached to native government	Detached from foreign government
Displaced home base	Permanent home base
Capitalist controlled	Imperialist controlled
Politically oppressed	Politically oppressed
Economically oppressed	Economically oppressed
Culturally oppressed	Culturally oppressed
Educationally oppressed	Educationally oppressed
Product of racism	Product of racism

BLACK GHETCOLONY

Homogeneous ethnic population
Controlled by native government
Capitalist controlled
Politically oppressed
Economically oppressed
Culturally oppressed
Educationally oppressed
Product of racism

The diagram which I have outlined is no attempt to play with semantics. Instead, it represents a concern to identify the forces which oppress the black community. The word, ghetcolony, then, delineates a community that is the product of oppression and reveals the manifestations which perpetuate it. An examination of this diagram will show that there are three dominant systems which are responsible for the oppression in the black ghetcolony.

Capitalism——Racism——Colonialism
Black Ghetcolony

These systems are all interrelated and though individually they do contribute to the oppression of other groups, black people are the only group in this country which is victimized by all three. This is an important distinction to make because all too often we tend to lump black people together with the Indians, Chicanos and more recently the indigent white Americans. However, the oppression of black people is far more pervasive, for it spans the full range of oppressive systems which make up the power structure in America.

With this brief analysis of the system of oppression, we now have a frame of reference to help us better understand how the community of North Lawndale has become just another black ghetcolony.

Chicago is filled with black ghetcolonies.

They can also be found in Garfield, Kenwood, Englewood, Woodlawn, Grand Crossing and the dozens of welfare housing prisons which are built to accommodate the disenfranchised. Historically, Chicago has always been a Dante's inferno for black people. Beneath its veneer of liberalism lies the most flagrant racism of any large northern city. The fact that Jean Baptiste Point DuSable, a black man, was the first non-Indian to settle here is of little significance when one weighs the lowly political and economic status of Chicago's black community. Although black people make up over one third of the city's population and constitute Chicago's largest ethnic group, they find themselves the most abused, the most powerless and the most exploited of any group in the city.

In Chicago, the system of oppression is nurtured by a well-organized political machine and a cadre of businessmen who sit on interlocking board structures which make the major decisions in this city. As one would expect, black people play no important role in this system and merely function as subordinates within it. A study published by the Chicago Urban League in 1968 clearly shows the disparity of this pecking order.

> The powerlessness of Negroes is manifested in
> their current inability to make and enforce
> decisions for their own communities or to have
> significant influence in shaping public and
> private programs, large institutions or the
> society's direction and purpose.[1]

This study surveyed major insitutions, both private and public, in the Chicago area to ascertain what percentage of black people held key policymaking positions. Its results were anything but encouraging, and can best be summed up by the following statement.

> Therefore, it is safe to estimate that Negroes
> held less than one percent of the effective
> power in the Chicago metropolitan area.[2]

Although these findings were reported in 1968, there is no reason to believe that they have changed to any marked degree. While some token jobs have been assigned to a few blacks since this report, it is apparent that their influence to improve conditions in the black ghetcolony has not yet surfaced. Chicago's black ghetcolonies are still controlled by a white power structure which refuses to yield to the needs of black people.

And at the helm of this political and economic dynasty is Mayor Richard J. Daley who has done little to correct this situation. Under the despotic leadership of Mayor Daley, two generations of black youths have grown up without any marked improvements in their environment. But Mayor Daley continues to ignore this miscarriage of city government and, in his belligerent manner, prefers to boast about Chicago's picturesque skyline and its modern expressways which span most sections of the city.

But North Lawndale is real.

It has a reality so stark that words cannot really describe it. North Lawndale has to be seen, felt and smelled before one can even begin to understand what it is actually like. And, of course, sightseeing buses do not tour its cluttered streets, nor are there scenic postcards to show its inescapable poverty which stretches for nearly five and a half miles, and claims a population of over two hundred thousand black men, women and children.

The physical and social profile of North Lawndale is deplorable. Its statistics read like a survey that has been taken of a war-torn community:[3]

- Out of 30,243 total housing units, 34.1 percent are deficient and 14.0 listed as substandard.
- Most of the housing is over forty years old.
- Over 700 total housing units are lacking some or all plumbing.
- Less than 35 percent of its population have completed high school.
- Over 5,000 families are under the poverty level.
- The unemployment rate is among the highest in Chicago.
- Health conditions and sanitation rank among the poorest in Chicago.

As revealing as these figures are, they do not even begin to reflect the untold amount of deprivation that exists in North Lawndale. Social scientists have yet to develop an instrument that is sophisticated enough to measure human suffering.

North Lawndale was not always a black ghetcolony.

Prior to World War II it had been inhabited by Irish, Poles, and Jews, although the last group made up the largest constituency. But when the first mass of blacks began to take residence in North Lawndale around 1950, these white ethnic groups sought to find "safer" pastures. But this is a common pattern when blacks move into an all white community: a great influx of blacks automatically brings about a greater exodus of whites. It is an old American tradition.

The first migration of blacks to North Lawndale was, for the most part, of southern origin, and consisted of people thoroughly unaccustomed to the trauma of urban life. Undoubtedly they came in search of a better standard of living than what they had experienced in the South. But relocation does not always assure people of improving their status when they are black. Although the code of segregation is less explicit in the North, it still achieves the same results. The southern black migrants quickly and painfully learned that the protocol of northern urban life was far from what they expected. Yet, still they emigrated and North Lawndale was never again to be the same.

Although many of these early black families owned homes, because of the depreciation of the community after 1960, homeowners became fewer, slum lords more abundant and building inspectors less observant. As Black people began to heavily populate North Lawndale, Chicago's dual housing standards were hastily implemented.

That North Lawndale was to become a ghetcolony was inevitable.

After the great exodus of whites, North Lawndale began to take a sharp decrease in economic stability and general appearance. Apartments that once accommodated one family were dissected into multi-quarters, thereby making it possible for more families to utilize the same space. Also there was a noticeable decline in public services such as regular sanitation pick ups, street cleaning, preservation of parks and trees and other types of maintenance services a community needs to look presentable. And the political structure of North Lawndale, though it began to have some black representation, was still controlled by white politicians who resided outside the community. And these few black politicians seemed to lack the power to make changes, or perhaps, their lack of activity was influenced by the political machine which they religiously supported.

Traditionally this machine has been in the deceptive hands of the Democrats who have controlled it with vigorous force since the days of the presidential era of Franklin Delano Roosevelt. As a political party, which has been able to mesmerize black people into voting the straight Democratic ticket, with its empty promises, the Democrats take North Lawndale for granted. During most local and national campaigns, North Lawndale is so deluged with Democratic posters that one would think the Democrats were the only political party which existed. And on election days, its army of precinct workers protect this tradition by using unscrupulous tactics to assure that their candidates always receive an overwhelming plurality. However, if one was to closely scrutinize each cast ballot against the official voters registration roll he would, undoubtedly, discover that North Lawndale is one of the city's largest depositories for the storage of "ghost votes." This clandestine situation becomes even more scandalous when one takes into account the many other voting irregularities which are reported in North Lawndale during elections.

Once North Lawndale did seem to be on the brink of achieving some degree of political integrity. This occurred during the career of Benjamin Lewis, Alderman of the 24th Ward, a grass roots politician, who many believed was beginning to dislodge himself from the Daley machine as well as intervene in the previously undisturbed activities of the crime syndicate. Having successfully gained the support of a large constituency in North Lawndale, Alderman Lewis had begun to seek the job as Congressman of the Seventh District to further enhance his power. But on the evening of February 27, 1963, Alderman Lewis was mysteriously slain, gangland style, in his office at Roosevelt and Homan. Alderman Lewis' associate, George Collins, then claimed the title as North Lawndale's top black politician and in November 1970 became the first black Congressman of the Seventh District. Congressman Collins' political career drew mixed feelings. Though he was generally liked in North Lawndale, his politics seldom deviated from the politics of the regular Democratic machine. On December 8, 1972, Congressman Collins met an untimely and tragic death, in an airplane crash near Midway Airport on Chicago's South Side. His wife, Cardiss Collins, became the Democratic machines's popular choice to fill the vacancy left by her husband, and in a special election she had little trouble winning over her opponents.

North Lawndale remains a classic example of plantation politics. Despite an increase in black politicians, its political posture has all of the characteristics of the Daley machine. The President of the 24th Ward Regular Democratic Organization is still white, although, in recent years, blacks have gained a few ward committeemen positions and held four out of six state representative jobs. But most of these men are machine-oriented politicians who have yet to mount any programs which can challenge the system of plantation politics in North Lawndale. And despite the fact that two National Black Political Conventions have been held, the political scene in North Lawndale has not changed at all. In fact, its dismal outlook only helps to support the position held by some that politics, under the present political structure, will never be accountable to black people. Whether or not North Lawndale will support black politicians who will not placate machine politics remains uncertain. In the wake of the increased interest in black independent politics, North Lawndale has had a few black politicians who seem determined to bring honest government to the community. But these courageous men will need more than their stamina to change the corrupt political climate in North Lawndale. The people, too, must begin to flex their muscles and be accountable for their actions.

North Lawndale is filled with people.

Overpopulation is one of its most visible features. People seem to be everywhere. But overpopulation is always predictable when people are forced to live in restricted areas that come into being as the result of non-compliance to fair housing laws and the racist tradition of gerrymandering oppressed people. And as is true of any overpopulated area, where the level of human resources fails to keep pace with the needs of its growing population, there is bound to develop a condition that propagates slum housing, poor sanitary conditions, increased incidents of crime and a noticeable amount of deprivation. When schools become overcrowded and lack proper educational facilities; when public and private agencies hampered with the disease of bureaucracy; when political organizations controlled by people whose loyalties belong to people other than those they are supposed to represent and serve; when law enforcement agencies overreact to the normal frustrations that are sympathetic of suppression; and, when the business hierarchy bleeds a community of its limited finance without sharing any of its profits, then social rigor mortis sets in and the community assumes a deflated posture. While slums are in the long run costly to many people, they do, however, help a gluttonous few to live in regal comfort. And they are perpetuated by those who profit from their existence.

The early history of North Lawndale shows that it was once a thriving business community whose roots added considerably to the economic development of Chicago. A few of its economic milestones were the Central Park Theater, the first of a long line of movie houses built by Balaban and Katz, and the beginning of the

Marshall Field Company which opened its first retail store in North Lawndale, after having left the street merchant district around Halsted and Maxwell Streets commonly known as "Jew Town." North Lawndale is also the location for the Sears, Roebuck and Company national offices and main warehouses. And some of the city's oldest Jewish synagogues were located in North Lawndale. Along Douglas Boulevard, with its median strip of grass separating the street which connects Douglas Park with Garfield Park, these places of Jewish worship still stand, but have now been converted into Baptist and Methodist churches. And Roosevelt Road, which once accommodated many retail and wholesale stores and was one of the city's important commercial thoroughfares, is still a major artery. But the commerce which had flourished on Roosevelt Road is now gone and the shadow of decay has fallen upon its once thriving economy.

The decline of North Lawndale conformed to the pattern set by other ghetcolonies in Chicago when they, too, began to feel the economic vacuum left by fleeing white businesses.

White merchants began withdrawing around 1960. At first there were only a few, but as the symptoms of deprivation began to creep in, the number of businesses reduced considerably. This included most of its banks and other economic enterprises a community needs to preserve some semblance of economic stability. But it was the riots of 1966 and 1967 which completed the demise of the few large businesses which had remained.

"Black Power!"

"Freedom Now!"

"Burn Baby Burn!"

Like the anguished cries of a wounded tiger, these words resounded with a fury that made earlier calls for justice rather pale. For a brief moment black people in North Lawndale had found a way to express their true frustration. To many burning and looting became a natural alternative to their unanswered needs. And though it was black people who suffered the most during these uprisings, their wounds were beginning to be felt by other groups in Chicago who, heretofore, showed no concern for the black ghetcolony. Those who had previously exploited North Lawndale began to realize that they could no longer reap their harvest without sharing some of the pain which is borne by the people who are the consumers of exploitation.

While the social experts were, alledgedly, taken by surprise by the holocaust of Watts, they could not hide behind this same "cop out" when North Lawndale erupted in rebellion. Any fool could have predicted the events which turned North Lawndale into an incendiary battlefield. Although these uprisings touched other black ghetcolonies in Chicago, it was on the West Side that they were most vividly expressed.

On each occasion the forces of law and order were quickly and methodically put into execution. After the police were unable to harness these uprisings during their early stages, Mayor Daley appealed to the Governor for re-inforcements, and while the flames were still flickering in the sky, National Guardsmen were hurried into North Lawndale. With fixed bayonets illuminating their presence, guardsman boldly patrolled the streets with the vigilance of battle tested combat veterans. And to insure that these foot soldiers would not be harrassed by missiles and sporadic sniper fire, the army obligingly sent along jeeps and armored trucks, with fifty calibre machine guns hoisted on them, to deter such acts. North Lawndale was placed under martial law and, for a brief period, many black people began to realize that the police state was not just a fabrication of their imagination, but a reality.

After the flames had been smothered and the cries of discontent calmed, North Lawndale began the task of trying to rebuild itself. However, the job of rebuilding is much more arduous and North Lawndale, like other black ghetcolonies throughout America, found itself trying to replenish what it never had, a taste of freedom.

In their efforts to accomplish this almost impossible task, it became obvious to many North Lawndale residents that a new type of community organizational structure had to be developed, if their needs were to be met. Neither the traditional and conservative-minded community block clubs, the politically controlled Urban Progress Center nor the then dominant community organization, Greater Lawndale Conservation Commission, seemed sufficiently motivated to bring about needed improvements in North Lawndale. These groups had already been remiss in their accountability, and, in 1967, the Lawndale Peoples Planning Committee was established as a vehicle for community self-determination and community improvement. Later the Lawndale Peoples Planning Committee merged with the West Side Federation, an umbrella group, and the Lawndale Union to End Slums. The merger resulted in the formation of the Lawndale Peoples Planning and Action Conference (LPPAC) which later formed the North Lawndale Economic Development Corporation to be its economic arm and a model for change through large scale redevelopment activity. The formation of LPPAC was, indeed, a unique undertaking. In a community torn by dissension and mistrust, it was not easy to bring together divergent groups. However, at its inception, LPPAC was successful in attracting most groups in North Lawndale, although some leaders from these groups exploited LPPAC for their own vested interests.

Prior to the merger, two consulting firms, Greenleigh Associates, Inc. and Marcou O'Leary and Associates were hired by Lawndale Peoples Planning Committee to make a comprehensive study of North Lawndale, and to develop an action program for constructive community change. The findings of these firms produced a major plan for the redevelopment of North Lawndale. But then intra-group friction ensued, power struggles developed and political subterfuge set in. As a result of this chaos, LPPAC has suffered from the lack of steady leadership and organizational difficulties which have prevented it from achieving its potential. However, while LPPAC has yet to make a significant impact on the community, there are encouraging signs that the North Lawndale Economic Development Corporation will achieve some of its goals. The economic development corporation proposes to construct and manage a seventeen acre shopping center to be completed in 1976 and owns 95 acres of land to be developed as an in-city industrial park. Other projects on NLEDC's docket include application for a Cable Television franchise, a Health Care Park, financial institution and housing development.

In the area of housing, the most noticeable improvement has been in the rehabilitated homes managed by the Douglas Lawndale Corporation, a non-profit grass roots organization founded in 1970 by the Department of Urban Renewal. The Douglas Lawndale Corporation has already rehabilitated two hundred and forty units and constructed seventy-two new units. The goal of Douglas Lawndale Corporation is to refurbish all the homes and property along Douglas Boulevard to make that area exemplary of what can be achieved when the proper funds and resources are provided. But even if this admirable project is successful, it will do very little to counteract the pervasive poverty which grips most of North Lawndale. A few other homes have been improved by Lawndale Union to End Slums which was organized in 1966 when Dr. King came to North Lawndale to help correct its wretched housing.

Two other active community groups include the Lawndale Association for Social Health and the Westside Association for Community Action. The Lawndale Association for Social Health was founded in 1966 to help improve conditions in North Lawndale. Its more successful activities have been its training programs in carpentry and general construction for unemployed men. The Westside Association for Community Action (WACA), a coalition of most westside community organizations and agencies, has during its short development, attempted to deal with most of the social problems that beset North Lawndale. However, while it understands the problems and, in some cases, offers solutions to them, WACA lacks the kind of power that is needed to effectively alter the system of oppression.

Today, despite the many city, state and federal crises programs, which were promised after these "unofficial states of emergencies," empty lots and abandoned buildings still comprise much of North Lawndale. North Lawndale still looks as though it is in a state of riot. Its landscape remains tarnished and barren, its housing fatigued and dilapidated. But the promises continue to come and the people of North Lawndale patiently wait and hope that some day the "great American Dream" will visit it one night and heal its bruises.

North Lawndale is an ominous symbol of American injustice and those who suffer the greatest are its black children who spend most of their time learning how to cope with an oppressed environment so that they can only grow up to be oppressed adults. For it is within this turbulent climate that black children must develop coping skills to survive the daily tribulations that confront oppressed people. The pre-adolescent years make up the most crucial period in the human development life cycle. It is the time when an individual begins to carve out his set of values, mold his attitudes and unravel his identity. Yet, the black child in North Lawndale receives little support as he wanders through this most difficult of journeys. And the system of oppression that he lives under only perpetuates the problems which stifles his chances to become a self-actualizing person.

SOCIAL OPPRESSION OF BLACK GHETCOLONY CHILDREN

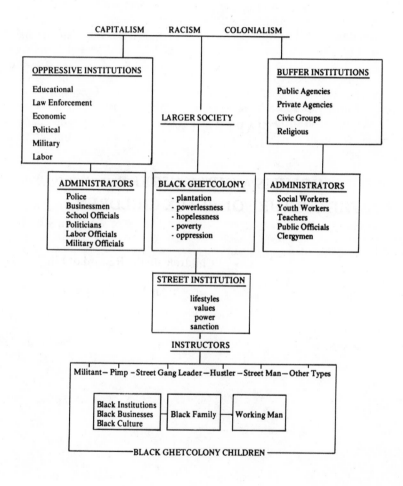

CHAPTER TWO

HOME IS A DIRTY STREET:
THE CULTURE OF BLACK CHILDREN

"Children are the Reward of Life"

An African Proverb

Summer mornings in North Lawndale never appear to change. They quickly become a part of ghetcolony tradition.

A pervasive episode of hopelessness and poverty.

What was true yesterday is more than likely to be true today.

There are the same decrepit structures basking under the sun with their frayed window shades half drawn, and the odor of hominy grits, fried pork and burnt toast seeping out into the almost death-like air. On hot days one can see fatigued ebony faces protruding out of windows to gain relief from the morning humidity.

And the stenchy alleys covered with broken wine bottles, empty beer cans, urine, and the feces of stray dogs and unwanted people.

And the weary people waiting on street corners to catch the crowded buses which takes them to work.

And the school aged children who leave home before they have eaten breakfast.

And the whimpers of babies who are still hungry from yesterday's shortage of milk.

And the dispossessed men who mill in front of taverns waiting to quench their hunger with anything that can help them escape their pain and frustration.

And the hustlers, pimps, street men and other social outcasts who serve as models for the young.

And the blue signal light of a police squadron flashing down the street or the blaring of a fire truck answering a call of distress.

And there are the dirty streets.

Always the dirty streets.

Where ghetcolony children make their home.

A home that has an asphalt floor, tenements for its walls and a door which locks them in from the rest of the world.

Let's begin to look at a few of these oppressed children.

At 15th and Kedvale three boys are lagging pennies on a sidewalk in K-Town. Their ages are nine, ten and twelve. Younger aged boys are playing softball in the streets, and shouting and darting around the passing cars which monentarily disrupt their game. A group of little girls are skipping rope near a two story frame house, whose wooden shingles have begun to corrode from years of neglect. In the backyard a fat woman, wearing a tight bathrobe that pinches her body, is hanging the morning laundry. In front of the corner tavern, two old men begin arguing over a bottle of wine. The boisterous voices of other men can be heard inside. A teenage youth enters and after a few minutes comes out with a small brown bag which fails to cover the neck of a quart beer bottle he has tucked under his arm. A small boy, age four, dashes across the street and a

speeding car comes to a screeching halt, inches away from the
undisturbed child. A police squadron pulls over to the curb and two
officers get out, guns in hand, and enter a four story building. A few
people mill around the squadron and some of the kids begin to play
with the spotlight on the vehicle. The officers finally return with a
young adult male, his wrists handcuffed behind him, and
immediately leave before more people arrive.

It is a summer morning in North Lawndale and the streets are
active as usual.

The nine year old boy lags his coin and anxiously watches it
bounce around until it stops short of the crack in the sidewalk, that
serves as the marker for this popular ghetcolony contest.

"I win...mine's closes'."

"You mus' cain't see good nigga! Mines is."

The twelve year old boy takes issue with both.

"Y'all quit arg'n. I win."

"Shit man, you ain't got no eyes!"

"I can see better'n ya momma."

"Man don' talk about ma momma."

"Le's measure..."

The nine year old boy kneels and lays his fingers between each
coin to ascertain which is closest to the line. About this time two
older youths, ages fourteen and fifteen, walk up and without
provocation, one of them grabs the three pennies.

"Lea' dem alone. Dey ain' yo'rs," bristles the ten year old boy
who tries to retrieve his coin.

"Gimme my penny...you black nigga," he grimaces.

"Fuc' yo'sef punk," sneers the fifteen year old, "it ain' yo's
now."

The second older youth intervenes.

"Com'on man an' lea' dese sissies alone."

"Ya momma's a sissy," retorts the ten year old boy.

"Look ya li'l sonafabitch, I'll kick yo' ass!"

The younger boys begin to withdraw, voicing more obscenities
as they do.

"Git dat smart mothafuckah," cries one of the older boys as he
attempts to grab the ten year old.

"Fuhgit it man. Fuc' dem li'l pricks."

The younger boys have wisely distanced themselves across the
street in a vacant lot. There they hurl rocks and taunt their
adversaries. But the older boys ignore them and proceed onward,
with pennies in hand.

The younger boys remain in the lot rock tossing at various
objects as they let off steam.

"My brotha'll take care o'dem," pouts the ten year old as he misses a beer can. "I know where dey live.' "

"Yeah an' you know dey liv' 'cross Pulaski in Vice Lords territory too," reminds the twelve year old. "Yo' brotha don' har'ly wanna mess wi' dem."

"Fuc' dem man. . .my brotha's in da Cobras!"

"I tho't 'e wuza Gestapo."

"Naw man dey don't do shit but smoke pot."

"You eva smoke pot?"

"Yeah—once," comments the ten year old.

"Ha di'ja feel?"

"I fo'got man." He scratches his head in jest. Laughter follows.

"I once took a Christmas tree," boasts the nine year old.

"Man you musta been outta yo' min'."

"He crazy anyway man."

"Ya momma's crazy!"

"Fuc' you man an' yo' momma."

"Hey—you 'member Johnny Otis? "E wuz in our room las' year."

"You mean da dude da' swung at da princ'pal?"

"Yeah man, dat crazy dude."

"E tried ta mess wi' me one time, but I tol' im t' cool it."

"Yeah. . .well 'e died man, from takin' one o' dose pills."

"You betta be cool from now on."

"Yeah, be cool or be a fool. . .a dead fool."

After exchanging more dialogue the three boys proceed to the school playground. There they join other boys in throwing rocks at the few remaining school windows which have not yet been broken from the annual missile assault that claims hundreds of windows each summer.

"I wish Mistuh Miles wuz in dat room," jokes the twelve year old boy as he reels back like a major league baseball pitcher. "I'd hit im sure 'nough."

"Ain't his fault you flunked."

"Aw dat mothafuckah wuz jus' prejudice, da's all. An' anyway 'e wuz nothing but a fag wit' all dat sissy hair.

"Ya just stupid. Dat's why yo're still in de fifth grade." The ten year old pretends he's holding a baseball bat and swipes at a few imaginery pitches.

"I'm gonna be in his room next year. And if he mess wit me. . .he betta watch out."

"Yeah, and wat cha gonna do?"

"Ya see."

"Well at least Mistuh Miles don' give ya no homework like dat fat Mrs. Smith."

"Dats cause Mistuh Miles thinks we all dumb bells. He even said so hisself." The twelve year old hurls another rock which easily finds its mark.

"Man when we go back to school...ain't gonna be no windows."

The nine year old laughs as he demonstrates the accuracy of his arm with another direct hit.

"Don't nobody care anyway."

A police squardron drives up but the rock throwing continues. It is only when one of the policemen alights from the vehicle that the youths begin to fan out in all directions.

"Them damn black sons o'bitches! Can't even respect their own schools. No wonder they don't learn a damn thing." The officer gets back into the squad car as a couple of other youths across the street begin to jeer.

"They just don't know no better," replies the officer at the wheel. "What do you expect from a bunch of savages. Nobody's teachin' 'em any manners."

The squadron's blue emergency signal lights up and the car speeds away to answer one of the many calls it will undoubtedly make during the day.

The three boys have, by this time, drifted to the corner of Sixteenth and Pulaski, a busy intersection. They just mill around and observe the activities of various people. Often when a bus stops at the corner, they make faces at the passengers.

For lack of anything to do, they have nothing to do.

Then they begin playing in front of the restaurant which is diagonally across from the currency exchange. One boy picks up a stick and begins poking another, as if he were a dashing caballero.

"Aw stop it man," comments the boy who is being pricked in the ribs.

"Wha'sa matta, ya scared? Cain't you defen' yo'se'f?" He continues to jump around with the make believe weapon.

"You betta quit it 'fore I knock da shit outta you!"

"Hey le's play cowboy," suggests the ten year old.

"O.K., I'm Jesse James."

"I'm Billy da Kid," exclaims another."

"I'm 'o be Matt Dillon, da fas'est gun in da Wes'."

" 'E ain't fas' as Wyatt Earp."

"Bat Mas'erson's da fas'est. I seen 'im kill six guys wit' one gun. Da's my man."

"I bet John Wayne could out shoot 'im."

"John Wayne ain' shit. 'e's jus' in da movies."

By this time the proprietor of the restaurant has come to the door. His furious eyes complement his firm voice.

"O.K. you guys. Ain't you got anything else to do but hang around here. This ain't no place for monkey business."

"Fuhgit you," shouts the twelve year old boy.

"I'm givin' you one minute!" He holds his hand in a clenched position.

"Don' nobody wanna stay aroun' 'ere anyway!"

"Yea, we don' hav' ta play in fron' o' yo' dirty sto'e."

"It's you boys that keep it dirty."

"You could sweep da flo'r sometime."

"I'm warning you!"

The boys run and begin playing in a nearby lot that is filled with striped cars which they improvise as props for their shenanigans. They play for about an hour, re-enacting all of the famous western scenes they have seen on television or at the movies. They perform the gunfight at the O.K. Corral twice; the slaying of Jesse James; dozens of high noon shootouts; battles with hostile Indians; and, they even add some modern-day techniques to their make-believe world.

At noon, the temperature rises considerably and after the boys finish killing each other off, they walk leisurely down Pulaski Road. generally considered to the restraining line for Cobras and Vice Lords. The boys live west of Pulaski Road in K-Town, which is in Cobra territory. The area was given that name because most of the streets begin with the letter K. Seldom do the boys cross over to Vice Lord territory.

"Le's go swimmin' at Franklin Park," suggests the nine year old.

"An' let dem studs rip off my clothes?" returns the ten year old.

"Man don' nobody want dem rags you wearing."

"Ya momma might."

"Ya momma might wan' me to bus' som' a dem naps off yo' head too."

"My hair's better'n yo's nigga;"

"Man what you talkin' 'bout'. All niggas got bad hair."

Yea, but at leas' da comb don' break when I comb it."

"Why don'tcha getta fry like Big Daddy?"

"You know da ol' saying," adds the nine year old.

"Conkaline rules da worl'

Not a kink not a curl

It may turn red
But da roots ain' dead
It may turn brown
But it still lays down."
They begin to laugh and slap each other's hands.
"Two cen's fo' some skin."
"Yea put it dere."
"But wha' about da swimmin' man. Dem studs ain' go' mess
wit us if we stay tagetha."
"I don' wanna go swimmin' dere anyway. All dat glass and dem
studs peein' in da wata."
"You jes don' wanna show yo' pussy."
"Fuc' you man. You ain' neva had a piece noway."
"Un huh. . .I got some from ya momma, da's why you here."
"Yo' momma's a who'e an' I metta at da door an' she got so'e
'cause I wouldn't give'r no mo'e."
"Yea, well I fucked yo' motha in da Brookfield Zoo. Gave'r so
much she di'n' know what to do."
"Cain't you cats stop all dat sigin', "intervenes the twelve year
old. "Le's go to da Boys Club."
"Ain't nothin' ta do dere but play ping pong. And dem
counselors is always hollerin' at somebody."
"Da's 'cause dey think dey so much betta."
"I use ta belong dere, but dey always tellin' ya what ta do."
"Yea man. . .jus' like school."
"It's a drag man."
"I know. . .le's go ta Rufus' house."
"Is 'e outta St. Charles?"
"Man 'es been out two weeks. Where you been?"
"He's always gettin' in trouble. Prob'bly make us break into
somebody's house."
"Wha's wrong wit' dat? We'll make a li'l money."
"You mean two bits. I ain' doing 'is dirty work fo' nothin'."
"De last time I went out wit dat dude he made me break into ole
Mistuh Johnson's T.V. Shop."
"Dat's when ya got caught. . .ain't it?"
"Ya betta believe it. After I got in de back door, Mistuh
Johnson woke up and came out wit dat big shotgun of his. Man
I didn't know what ta do."
"Yea I bet cha reall' blew yo cool."
"Wasn't funny man. I spent one nite in da Audi Home. Dat
place is jus lika jail."
"I know what cha mean baby. I bin dere three times myself."

"Well I don't wanna go dere agin. De judge will send me to St. Charles sur nough I'm standin' here."

"At least dey feed you dere man."

"I'm hungree," comments the nine year old.

"Don cha momma ever feed ya?"

"Don't make him feel bad. Ya know wat his momma is. I gotta few coins...let's go to Henry's on Roosevelt Road."

The boys reach Roosevelt Road. They stand around for a few minutes before going to the hamburger stand. One of the boys buys a bag of french fries and smothers them with catsup. The other hands quickly find the greasy bag.

Across the street an unmarked police car pulls up along the curb where five older youths are standing. Two detectives jump out, revolvers in hand, and order the youths to face a nearby wall and spread their arms and legs. One of the detectives finds something beneath the shirt of one of the youths. The youths are then shoved into the car and sped away.

The boys finish the french fries. It is now 2:00 P.M.

They split up. Two proceed to Rufus' house while the third remains standing on Roosevelt Road gazing at his world.

A world of neglect and dirty streets.

Dirty streets which wind through North Lawndale like malignant arteries leaving despair and tragedy on each block.

Home is a dirty street and the black child must learn to live on it the best he can. More than likely he will spend the remainder of his life walking up and down its crumbled pavement.

We could expound on these boys' experiences and follow them for the remainder of the day, until darkness has crept in and most people have gone to bed. But the story might become somewhat repetitious or monotonous, to hear these young boys engage in verbal obscenities, throw rocks, romanticize stories, talk about gangs, exhibit their toughness and fears as they walk along the dirty ghetcolony streets. But this type of exposition would not explain why they behave as they do. It would not even begin to describe why most children in North Lawndale have already been destroyed before they are born because this society has systematically laid a foundation for them that is so fragile it collapses with the slightest provocation.

Most people will, no doubt, label the behavior of the children whom I have just described as being the manisfestations of a sub-culture. However, this is another term which I find misleading. A sub-culture implies that it is a deviant response to a larger culture whose values are being repudiated for various reasons. But the culture of the ghetcolony is not a reaction to the larger culture that oppresses it but a distinct conglomerate of values that has been shaped by its own necessity to cope with oppression. The culture of the ghetcolony is a *coping one* because its development and formation are organized around survival needs. The behavior of the three boys only reveals how black children develop coping mechanisms to deal with conditions in their environment that have been imposed on them by the system of oppression.

Throughout America black children who live in the hellish squalor of our black inner city ghetcolonies, like North Lawndale, are constantly faced with a myriad of social pressures that stigmatize them with irrevocable scars and the nebulous feeling of not knowing what their destinies hold for them. The black inner city child is a member of a coping culture which, as W. E. B. DuBois states, "yields him no true self-consciousness, but only lets him see himself through the revelation of the other world." And the other world for black children happens to be white America, a hostile society that has historically treated black people like lepers and done everything possible to degrade their minds, enslave their bodies and dehumanize their rights as human beings. While the polemics of war, revolution, pollution, cybernation, abortion and free love take priority over their welfare, these children continue to compose the most neglected minority in a society where they are also members of the most oppressed minority. They are, in fact, victims of oppression who must grow up in this most inimical and violent of societies receiving little positive guidance from either adults or social institutions. And so black ghetcolony children learn to survive in the only institution which is sympathetic to their plight; the institution of the streets.

CHAPTER THREE

THE STREET INSTITUTION: SURVIVAL SCHOOL FOR BLACK CHILDREN

It is the underprivileged Negro Child about whom we are concerned. For it is this child upon whom the ultimate success of our race depends. We must salvage from the wreckage this down-and-out group and lift it to a higher plane of civilization if we as a group are to survive and live on into the future.

The Education of the Negro Child
Dista Caldwell

The streets of North Lawndale constitute an institution in the same way that the church, school and family are conceived as institutions. They all have a set of values and norms to govern and re-enforce their existence. Of course, the social structure of the street lacks the sophistication these other institutions have. Nevertheless, it is an institution because it helps to shape and control behavior. And it is on the streets where the black child receives his basic orientation to life. The streets become his primary reference because other institutions have failed to provide him with the essential skills he needs to survive in the ghetcolony. And for a child to survive the ghetcolony he must undergo a rigorous apprenticeship that will enable him to compensate for the lack of guidance from other institutions and adults. He becomes a student of the "asphalt jungle" because that is where he can learn the skills he needs.

When black children are not compelled to attend school, and often when they are, they usually can be found in the streets. The streets become their text, instructor and subject matter. The curriculum for this asphalt institution incorporates many of the same courses that are found in the formal school setting: sociology, political science, history, biology and even the physical sciences. However, unlike the school, the courses in the Street Institution are structured around community norms and are more binding on its members.

Its sociology consists of studying the so-called pathology of the ghetto. Political science is learned from the unscrupulous exploits of corrupt politicians; history from years of discrimination and economic deprivation; biology from youths smoking marijuana and having sex in dirty alleys; and the physical sciences are taught by learning how to endure elements unfit for human consumption. And the theoretical references for the Street Institution reflect how the people actually live and not how others would like them to function. There are no semester breaks or summer vacations, for study in the ghetcolony is a continuous cycle which never stops, not even in the face of death.

The values of the Street Institution are shaped from the physical and psychological manifestations of the black ghetcolony. From these manifestations certain life styles are created that are exemplified by the instructors of the Street Institution. The instructors consist of hustlers, pimps, street men, militants, gang leaders and working men. And, though, these men do not have masters and Ph.D degrees, their credentials have been earned from actual experiences and not from the sterile laboratories of formal academic institutions. Although the black ghetcolony has other institutions, schools, public and private agencies, etc., these institutions, because of their affiliation with the larger society, have a different set of values. Thus, there is created a polarization of interest which is in constant conflict. And the people who are assigned with the responsibility of maintaining the values of the larger society are the administrators. The administrators are teachers, ministers, policemen, social workers, businessmen and public officials. However, it is the instructors who are the major influences in the ghetcolony and subsequently the Street Institution is shaped around their values and life styles. That is to say, the instructors are the models who the children learn from because the administrators have no affinity with the values of the ghetcolony. And the few who do usually repudiate them in favor of the larger society's set of values. As a result, the instructors of the ghetcolony rebel against the policies of the administrators and establish policies more appropriate for their survival. While the administrators try to regulate behavior, the instructors do everything possible to subvert the standards set by the larger society.

Few black ghetcolony children ever become full participants in the larger society, so therefore, they are motivated to achieve success within their own coping culture. Though they are exposed to the values of the larger society, through its administrators, these values are inaccessible to them and are, in fact, often the reasons why black children are oppressed. The ironic thing about the administrators is that while they try to superimpose the values of the larger society on the ghetcolony, they do very little to help black children obtain them. The so-called conventional norms of the larger society become unconventional in the black ghetcolony because the black ghetcolony has never been a part of conventional America. The mere fact that black people are still struggling to gain equality in this white-dominated society should attest to this. What the administrators fail to understand, or, for that matter, do not dare to accept, is that they represent the barriers which keep the black child isolated from the "mainstream."

As representatives of the larger society, they help to keep the black ghetcolony in a constant state of oppression. Their roles vary from the missionary (social worker), propagandist (school teacher), redeemer (minister), exploiter (businessman) lawmaker (politician) to the law enforcer (policeman). And it is all of these people who keep the black ghetcolony powerless.

As a student of the Street Institution, the black child cannot afford to lag behind. He must keep up with its demanding schedule, for his failure to do so only makes him more vulnerable to the oppressive elements in his environment. His early maturation is centered around becoming familiar with his community and learning how to manipulate it to serve his interest. The only passing grade is that of S for survival. He either survives or he does not. His classroom is his total environment, the alleys, pool halls, taverns, tenements and the streets on which he lives. By the age of twelve he has usually taken all the required courses, and is prepared to face the challenges which are thrust upon him. His entry into the street culture, as a full fledged member, is not certified by a diploma of achievement but, rather, by his proven ability to operate within the sanctions of his community. Graduation from the Street Insitution never comes for most. Instead, the black child spends the major portion of his life repeating the same courses, so that by the time he reaches adulthood it is almost impossible for him to change his orientation to life. He is caught in an endless cycle that seldom deviates.

The ghetcolony child automatically becomes a ghetcolony man.

The chain of oppression never breaks for each link is inextricably tied to the other.

How is the black child able to adjust to the Street Institution? His adjustment, for the most part, stems from his ability to develop certain coping skills which prepare him to meet the criteria for membership. He learns early in life that the street culture is his dominant influence and, therefore, begins to familiarize himself with its norms, values, social functions, and life styles, like any other student who seeks acceptance within a given institution. The coping skills that must be learned by the black child are *adaptability, verbal manipulation, role playing* and *how to interact* with his peers. These are his survival tools and the absence of any one only heightens the conflicts which he already has to face.

ADAPTABILITY

A remarkable thing about black children is their uncanny ability to adapt. Adaptability is a pre-requisite for survival in the ghetcolony. Without this skill, one quickly finds himself swallowed by the overpowering facets of ghetcolony life. The black child learns to adapt to a number of social inequities that normally would appear too demanding for his tender years. He must be able to deal with the oppressive forces which penalize his community as well as the negative forces coming from within. And his adjustment is made more difficult because of the inadequacies and the hypocrisy of formal institutions to provide him with positive guidance and a true perspective of his plight.

Social anthropologists tell us that the inability of a group to cope with its environment ultimately finds that group becoming extinct. This process of elimination is a law of nature which makes no compromises for those who are unable to survive because they lack the necessary coping skills. Neither does it show sympathy for those whose failure to gain these skills is through no fault of their own. Consequently, black children can look for little help from others and, therefore, must learn how to live or die through their own trial and error and hard knocks.

The adage, "when in Rome do as the Romans do," has its particular relevancy to the theory of adaptability. In its simplest interpretation it implies that for a person to survive in a culture he must learn to live like the culture's inhabitants. As the black child grows up he finds himself confronted with a set of demands and expectations with which he must learn to negotiate. And in his negotiations he learns what he can do and cannot do to remain a member in good standing. Unlike a tourist, who can leave Rome if he finds adaptability too painstaking, the black child has no way out and must make every effort to be "like the other boys" or develop defenses that can compensate for his lack of adaptability. If he chooses to withdraw, and few do, then he will be looked upon as some type of social freak and will find himself being the scapegoat of his community. The exclusion from the dominant culture patterns of the community could also cause him great anxieties and possibly serious psychological problems. The norm for social deviancy is often different in the black ghetcolony, and sometimes the child who tries to emulate so-called conventional behavior is seen as being more deviant than one who openly violates certain conventional sanctiond.

This is not to imply that all black children must and do adhere to the same lifestyle. There is diversity among them as there is with all human beings. But the dichotomy is relative or situationally oriented and not community mold. The black child must adapt to a number of inequities: slum housing, poor schools, economic deprivation, teenage street gangs, police brutality and various social stigmas. When one takes a penetrating look at these inequities, it becomes a miracle these "ghetcolony infants" overcome any of the obstructive forces which adulterate their young lives.

VERBAL MANIPULATION

The manner in which black children speak is often viewed with disdain, especially by the administrators. Black children are chastised, criticized and ridiculed for the way they talk and their language is called everything from "street talk" to just plain "bad grammar."

Yet, the language the ghetcolony child speaks is quite functional to him, for it allows him to reflect his enviroment as well as act as a stabilizer for threatening situations. This mode of language, i.e., street talk, hip talk, rapping, signifying or playing the dozens, consists of using words in such a manner that the mere phonics of them seems to transmit the cultural patterns of the ghetcolony. I choose to call this type of speech verbal manipulation instead of some of the other names it is commonly called, such as "substandard English," "improper English," or even "Black dialect." The latter term is generally used by many sociologists and educators as a rationalization to define its relationship to so-called standard English. However, this term to me is inappropriate because it denotes a way of speaking that is a derivative of a more correct language. But the language of black children is correct to them and need not be categorized as being substandard. Instead, it should be accepted as a natural way of speaking in view of the cultural origin of black people whose original language reflected a variety of sounds, none of which were English. And regardless of how much so-called standard English has been superimposed on black people, they have obviously retained some of the phonetics of their mother tongue. Because black people have never fully assimilated into the larger society, black children should not be expected to master the tongue of those who keep them oppressed. The primary language of any people should be a reflection of their own culture and not an imitation of another.

Granted, the phonics of ghetcolony street language differs from the speech patterns of so-called standard English, but this difference should not be confused with it being inferior. Black children do not speak so-called standard English because this language does not allow them the flexibility in speech they need to negotiate with situations in their environment. Instead, they make a choice between speaking a dysfunctional language and one which is more in harmony with the demands placed upon them for their survival. Obviously the black child's choice to speak the language that reflects his environment is not due to his lack of exposure to so-called standard English. He is constantly being exposed to so-called standard English through television, movies, public schools and other establishment institutions. But he makes no real effort to emulate so-called standard language because it acts as a conduit for articulating a way of life which is inconsistent with his own. However, he does extract from so-called standard English a frame of reference from which he then translates into his own mode of so-called standard English. It is radical only in the sense that the black child manipulates it to be functional to his needs. This is not to say that verbal manipulation influences the phonetic differences which typify the black child's translation of so-called standard English. As I have already noted, the phonics of street language must be viewed from a historical context if they are to be understood. When black people were brought to America as slaves they spoke a variety of indigenous tribal languages. Slaves were not taught so-called standard English but learned to speak it through their own curiosity and the realization that speaking their master's tongue was essential to their survival. Regardless of how hostile the plantation system was, slaves realized that their survival was predicated on their ability to negotiate with the dominant language spoken in their oppressed environment. Though most slaves were successful in making the transition from their native language to so-called standard English, this change was not accomplished without them retaining some of the phonics of their original language.

But black children are constantly being indicted for the way they talk.

"They just don't seem to be able to articulate properly."

"I can't understand a thing they're saying."

"They always seem to drop their T's."

When one places these critical remarks in a social context he may arrive at the dreadful conclusion that black children are not human.

Dr. Orlando L. Taylor, a noted black socio-linguist, feels that language is the basis for determining social beings and, therefore, the failure of the larger society to recognize the speech patterns of black ghetcolony children as being legitimate suggests that black people lack human qualities. In fact, to even have to make a case for the language black people speak is, in itself, a covert admission of this belief.

The use of verbal manipulation was discerned in the conversation between the three boys. Each time one of them was challenged by a situation he didn't want to deal with, he would circumvent the situation and create one of his own and thereby set up a new challenge. When the boys could not counteract the physical threat of the older youths they quickly changed the confrontation to a verbal one. In this manner, they could, at least, retaliate and get some satisfaction from their verbal insults, even though the older youths kept the money. In this transference of goals, the confrontation became verbal rather than physical.

While this technique may violate middle class protocol, it does allow the user the chance to negotiate on his own terms. When he is unable to cope with a situation on one level, he can transfer the situation to a level where he can be secure.

Many black youths do express themselves rather aggressively and take pride in doing so. But this kind of verbal expression is basically a reflection of how they cope with their environment. The formation of a language derives itself from the social motif of a people's culture and when that culture is tainted with the scars of poverty, social deprivation and oppression, then it is only natural for the language to reflect these manifestations. Black ghetcolony youths speak the language which is shaped by their environment and not because of any inherent physical or mental incapacity.

Verbal manipulation is also used to demonstrate how astute one is. The black child is impressed by cleverness, and when one has the ability to articulate in an impressive manner, he is looked upon as being "hip," "for real," "together," etc. To talk hip is to chauvinize one's awareness of the Street Institution. It adds glitter to the different ghetcolony lifestyles. A hip person knows what's happening and is able to articulate the latest "in group" expressions and cultural slang. He knows what to say, how to say it and when to say it. The hip talker avoids, whenever possible, physical confrontation, for he relies upon his skill with words to neutralize conflicting situations. Being able to "rap" in the ghetcolony is indeed an asset because it enables a person to verbalize his knowledge of the street culture instead of actually demonstrating what he learns or knows. That is to say, his ability to rap often compensates for having to prove physically that he is a learned student of the Street Institution.

A discussion on verbal manipulation would not be complete without commenting on the "dozens." Howard E. Seals in an essay entitled, "You Ain't Thuh Man Yuh Mamma Wuz" makes the following analysis of this popular verbal ghetcolony contest.

> The object in "the dozens" is to say the most uncomplimentary things one possibly can about the other person's female relatives: . . . yuh mamma . . . yuh snaggle-tooth gran'mammy . . . yuh hustlin' baby sister . . . ; all liberally sprinkled and punctuated with the expletive, "mothafuckah." The emotional tone to be maintained is that of hilariously, outrageously funny bantering. Some of the funniest turns of phrase that one can hear are to be heard between two black men "playin' thuh dozens."[2]

However, all dozens are not directed at the mother. Some are purely puns or insults exchanged between the contestants. When the female figure is used the dozens are more verbally aggressive and usually rely on obscenities to dramatize their effect. But the dozens are also a variation of signifying that allows for an exchange of expressions between two contestants to test which is the "hippest" and more verbally astute. An example of this type of exchange would be as follows:

Contestant One: Man you sure are ugly.

Contestant Two: If I had a face like yours...
                  I would buy me a gas mask.

Contestant One: Ya look like ya been in a fight
                  and only de other cat had a knife.

Contestant Two: Yeah if I looked like ya...
                  I would hide my face in de
                  toilet stool.

Although the analogies are often non-sensical, they have a poetic humor that makes them amusing and challenging. Such a contest will go on until one of the contestants concedes.

When the dozens is directed at the mother, they will go something like the following:

Contestant One: Yo momma's a man.

Contestant Two: Ya should know she fucked yo momma.

Contestant One: I saw yo momma on de railroad track
                  ...eating shit outta paper sack.

Contestant Two: Yo momma gotta shape dats out of
                  sight. Dats why she only comes
                  out at night.

Contestant One: I took yo momma for a car ride and
                  the car ride made her sick. Took
                  her home and put her to bed and
                  called for doctor dick.

Contestant Two: Man I fucked your momma in the
                  Brookfield Zoo and gave her so
                  many babies...she didn't know
                  what to do.

The dirty dozens will go on until one contestant gives in or changes the contest to a physical one, because he can no longer accept the verbal assault of his opponent. The dozens can be a dangerous contest to play and often causes intense animosities between contestants. However, these conflicts are usually shortlived and do not create permanent grudges.

Rodger D. Abrahams, in a study on black folklore in Philadelphia, suggests that the dozens are a latent reaction to the matriarchal structure of the black family and shows an impulsive resentment toward the mother figure.

> So he must in some way exorcize her influence.
> He, therefore, creates a playground which en-
> ables him to attack some other person's mother,
> in full knowledge that the person must come
> back and insult his own. Thus, someone else
> is doing the job for him, and between them they
> are castigating all that is feminine, frail, unmanly.[3]

Because Mr. Abraham's theory supports the traditional view-point of the black family, that it is woman dominated, he fails to take into account that boys with fathers also play the dozens, and it is not uncommon to see girls participating as well. However, Mr. Abrahams' data does not reflect these things and consequently the black family is, again, used as an object for interpreting street behavior without taking into consideration that, as Mr. Seals has suggested, "Playing the dozens attacks a key fantasy concerning feminism, specifically, the fantasy concerned with the mystical sanctity of motherhood." Mr. Seals feels that because the black woman is not seen as a goddess object, like her white counterpart, she is subject to the same type of verbal abuse as a man. This interpretation appears more valid because it does reflect how some black men relate to black women in the ghetcolony.

Another faulty analysis that Mr. Abrahams makes is that the dozens compensates for a lack of masculinity and permits its user to feel superior over women by degrading them with words.

> Through the 'dozens' the youth has his
> first real chance of declaring the dif-
> ferences between male and female and of
> taking sides in the struggle. The femin-
> ine world that has gripped and yet reject-
> ed him has been rejected in kind and by a complete
> negation. (It is not unusual
> for such complete rejection to occur
> toward something that has so nearly seduced
> us to its values.) Significantly, this
> first 'manly' step is done, with a
> traditional manly look, the power of words.
> Thus, this declaration of sexual
> awakening and independence also provides

> the youth with a weapon of sexual power,
> one which he will have to cultivate and
> use often.[4]

Once again, Mr. Abrahams amplifies stereotyped conceptions of black people. Doesn't he know that women also participate in the dozens and that the contest is not restricted to a homogeneous grouping? Also, it is high time to abort the ludicrous concept that black youths play the dozens to prove their masculinity. Black youths have no basic problem in identifying their masculinity. This ridiculous point of view is mainly the outgrowth of intellectual racism which has attempted to castrate the black male. The trouble with Mr. Abrahams' analysis is that he attempts to superimpose whites' interpretation of masculinity in making his judgment of black youth. What he is really saying, in fact, is that if black youths do not emulate white masculine models they cannot achieve masculinity by emulating black models.

The concern which should be shown is not whether or not black youths have difficulty in asserting their masculinity but rather are they being properly influenced by the male models which are in the ghetcolony. We must begin to understand that the black ghetcolony does not lend itself to creating Burt Lancasters, John Waynes, Cary Grants and other male models which are perpetuated as representing "American masculinity." Even though some blacks try to emulate these commercialized models, they quickly learn that the lifestyles of a Burt Lancaster, John Wayne and a Cary Grant do not make it in the black ghetcolony. Also, it is questionable if these models could ever begin to endure what most black males go through. Masculinity for black youths must be judged by the cultural norms of the black community and not by the norms of a commercialized movie industry.

However, the weakness of ghetcolony street language is that it loses its effectiveness or legitimacy when used in other environments. Formal institutions, such as the school, refuse to yield to a different set of standards. So when a black child employs this language in a school setting he is looked upon as being stupid, discourteous, arrogant or downright vulgar. Yet, it is often the only defense he has to deal with what to him is a hostile environment. He does not make a differentiation between the school and the Street Institution and, therefore, uses the language which is most functional to him. Consequently, the black child learns to speak a language which, for the most part, becomes dysfunctional outside of the ghetcolony. When he uses this language in the larger society, he finds that it does not gain for him the same benefits he receives in the ghetcolony.

Thus, he is penalized for deviating from so-called standard English and also made to feel that he suffers from some speech deficiency.

In recent years, black ghetcolony language has been glorified as being some exotic expression which captures the essense of true soul. Even the administrators will support this exoticism for it is a way of making oppressed people feel that they are blessed with some special qualities despite the fact they are victims of oppression. The language of the black ghetcolony does have a type of verve that characterizes many of today's cultural idioms. Its gusty vocabulary gives many people a feeling of being independent and "down to earth," both desirable attributes for the cultural fadist. Even the word "muthafucker" has gained wide acceptance in the larger society, although this negative word originated as the result of the slavemaster's rape of black women, it has become a favorite ghetcolony expression. Now it has been given an exotic flair that tends to glamorize its negativism. It is indeed unfortunate that black youths find this word to self-gratifying. While member of the larger society use it as a means to pretend that they can be "down to earth," black youths use the word as a means to cope with certain situations which they find oppressive and threatening. Therefore, the word "muthafucker" becomes a crutch to them which is used as a verbal declaration of their contempt for others and as a shield for their own frustrations.

But the administrators who glorify ghetcolony language make no effort to synthesize it into the formal institutions which they use for their credibility. The administrators will probably flaunt their versions of ghetcolony language at certain closed socials or at other places where the middle class gets "turned on," but they dare not speak it in front of their subjects. As the caretakers of white middle class values, they must, at all times, maintain their facade of superiority, and only speak the language which is expected of this breed. On the contrary, the black child speaks ghetcolony language as an indispensable means of communication for his survival, and not as a cultural vogue.

ROLE PLAYING

Children are great imitators.

They begin to mimic other people at a very early age. It is a way for them to learn how to function within the cultural patterns of their community. The world is a stage and children must learn how to be participants in its human drama. It is customary to call this learned behavior role playing; that is, behavior which imitates and emulates certain styles of life. Role playing fulfills many needs and acts as guidelines to help people to conform to the prescribed norms of their culture. This is extremely important for children because it is during the formative years that people begin to mold their behavior which, for most, will deviate little during their life cycles. Adults become who they are largely because of the roles they learned to play as children. And most ghetcolony children become ghetcolony adults because early in their lives they begin to enact those roles which are identified with ghetcolony models.

Roles are learned from various models that are shaped by cultural traditions. Since the black child is a product of a dual culture, his own and the one that oppresses him, he begins to wean out those roles which are dysfunctional and adopts only those roles that best equip him for survival. The roles which black children select from will generally be determined by the following models: (1) Romantic models, (2) Heroic models, (3) Conventional models and (4) Functional models.

ROMANTIC MODELS

Romantic models create those roles, such as the western heroes the boys were emulating, that tend to project images which are not functional to the cultural patterns of the ghetcolony. They are usually fictionalized versions of people who exist only in myth, folklore, fairy tales, television and the movies. While they do intrigue children, they rarely can be transfered to real life situations. The boy who played Billy the Kid cannot make that role operate for him in an urban setting. Billy the Kid may have been a "bad hombre" but he was the product of a small town in New Mexico and the forces which shaped his career differ from those that oppress the life of a black child. Other examples of Romantic models would include Superman, Batman, the Green Hornet and even James Bond. But as white models, they do not lend themselves to being transmitted to the realities of ghetcolony life.

Although black ghetcolony youths do indulge in romanticism, most do not allow their fanciful excursions to deceive them into believing that their real world is embroidered with a silver lining. They are intelligent enough to make this distinction because they know their survival depends upon their ability to "make it" where they actually live and not in some fantasy of their imagination.

HEROIC MODELS

The Heroic models usually serve as propanganda symbols to

encourage black children to identify with exceptional people who have excelled despite seemingly insurmountable obstacles.

Heroic models are emphasized by the larger society to make black children feel that they can become illuminating figures through mere perseverance and faith in the system. They serve as "symbols of hope" to indoctrinate black children to believe in the American Dream. A classic example of the heroic model is Abraham Lincoln, whose rise from log cabin to White House has been dramatized in every possible way to show that achievement in this society can be obtained regardless of one's economic or social status. Other models often used to perpetuate this myth are Thomas Jefferson, Benjamin Franklin and Babe Ruth. But these models represent white men who were not subjected to the same kinds of injustices which have oppressed black people.

And even when black Heroic models are used as examples of the "Horatio Alger" legacy, they, too, fall short in compensating for the lack of real opportunities available to black children. Men like Frederick Douglas, George Washington Carver, Booker T. Washington, and Paul Laurence Dunbar did, of course, overcome great barriers to achieve success. But these were extraordinary men whose talents far exceeded those of some of the white examples mentioned. Perhaps, if these exceptional black men had been really recognized for their talents, a Frederick Douglas would have become President, Paul Laurence Dunbar awarded a Pulitzer Prize, Booker T. Washington given the same prestige as Thomas Jefferson and the legend of Babe Ruth would have been surpassed by the athletic feats of the great black baseball player, Josh Gibson. While black Heroic models do, no doubt, inspire some black youths they, too, fail to be functional for the masses of black ghetcolony children. To a great extent these models only re-affirm what black children know already—that for a black person to make it in this society he has to almost be a facsimile of superman.

The larger society continues to propagandize "so-called" heroic models because it hopes that black children will feel that they can achieve success, regardless of their race or color. But the opportunity structure of America makes achievement at certain levels highly improbable for black children and, subsequently, Heroic models differ very little from Romantic models in that like the latter they are also a part of America's well documented fantasy of social equality.

CONVENTIONAL MODELS

Conventional models influence children to adhere to the

standards which society sets for most of its people. They serve as examples for the way people should behave in a society. As robots of the ruling class they are so programmed that their behavior is always predictable. They have been manipulated into accepting the status quo and rarely deviate from the social sanctions prescribed for them. Conventional models are expected to exemplify how loyal Americans should act, regardless of where they are placed on the list of national priorities. Still they are considered to be the cornerstones of America's so-called democracy and become the greatest conveyors of its propaganda.

Obviously conventional models are not functional in the black ghetcolony because black people have yet to achieve equal status and, therefore, conventional behavior does not gain them the same benefits, that white people receive. Because of the double standards in this country, black people are treated differently and must adopt alternative ways for coping with this cultural duality. Conventional models become dysfunctional to black people because their lives have been shaped by social standards which are vastly inconsistent with those assigned to members of the larger society.

Still most black children do, at one time in their development, attempt to emulate conventional models. But they eventually learn that conventional roles do not prepare them to deal with the unconventional elements in their environment and quickly repudiate them in favor of roles which are more functional to their survival. Indeed, it is fatuous for black children to try to behave like provincial Americans when the larger society denies them those avenues which are supposed to amalgamate them into the so-called mainstream.

FUNCTION MODELS

Black children must learn roles which allow them to perform on their stage, the black ghetcolony. They adopt functional roles because these are the roles which help them survive. Functional roles always take precedence over the others, for they are more in keeping with the cultural norms of the black ghetcolony and can be extended to one of the lifestyles which is exemplified by the street instructors.

The roles most prevalent among black children are (1) the Cool Cat, (2) the Jester, (3) the Square, (4) the Regular and (5) the Antagonist. While none of these roles is conclusive, they do represent cross patterns of lifestyles which black children adopt to cope with their environment.

THE COOL CAT

The Cool Cat is probably the most imitated of the lot. Being cool is very important in the ghetcolony. When things go down in the ghetcolony, such as intense police harassment, it is advantageous to be cool. When situations become "uptight", being cool is a trademark of street sophistication. Black children learn how to be cool under the most extenuating circumstances. Being cool also implies that one is "hip," "together," and is able to function under considerable pressure. It becomes a stabilizer that allows one to minimize threatening situations and ignore others which he cannot effectively deal with. It also accompanies a lifestyle that is personified by a neat appearance, skill in verbal manipulation and an uncanny ability to stay out of serious trouble.

The Cool Cat often appears indifferent to the problems around him, as though he is insensitive to pain, frustation or death. He rarely allows his real inner feelings to surface, because they may reveal that he is more sensitive to other people. The lifting of his protective shield would make him appear timid, and, therefore, dilute his image. The Street Institution has trained him to act in this manner, to be cool, stern, impersonal, in the face of all kinds of adversities.

THE JESTER

The Jester deals with situations in a different manner. Instead of being reserved like the Cool Cat, he engages in shenanigans to compensate for his weaknesses. He learns to behave foolishly, for comedy is often seen as an anecdote for problems he does not like to face head on. By being funny he is able to gain attention and, thus, achieve some status in the community. To maintain this role, he will allow himself to be a foil for other boys and is always prepared to participate in pranks and mischievous acts. Although he is not taken seriously, he possesses a great amount of nerve, for part of his function is to be a human guinea pig to experiment with new situations. Most jesters are followers and rarely become leaders.

The Jester will do almost anything to prove to his peers that he possess courage. Older boys will use him as a scapegoat to do their dirty work or "front him off" when it is to their advantage. Because he is so eager to be "one of the boys," he is easily manipulated and feels obligated to commit acts which ultimately find him in conflict with the law.

THE SQUARE

The Square is looked upon as a deviant because he does not adapt to certain street norms and resists being "a regular member of the Street Institution." His peers do not expect as much of him, as attested by these remarks:

"Johnny is a square so we won't ask him to have a drink with us."

"Billy doesn't know what's happening, so it ain't no sense taking him along."

While being a square places stigmas on a boy, it, nevertheless, guards him from engaging in certain types of behavior. A Square is not expected to do certain things and, therefore, he does not have to prescribe to all street norms. Occasionally the Square is identified as a "sissy," not due to any obvious feminine qualities, but rather because of his reluctance to accept certain challenges. Squares are even sometimes seen as being "good boys," but that is merely because they seem to stay closer to the conventional norms instead of the street norms.

The Square will not encounter as many problems with the administrators as the Cool Cat, Jester or the Antagonist, but he is constantly in conflict with his peers to maintain his own well being. He is usually excluded from being a member of a street gang and, as a result, has few friends to protect him from the gang's intimidation of non-gang members. Yet he must learn how to live among them, because his environment is the same as theirs and the social forces which influence their lives have an effect on his also. Because of this, the Square is more apt to experience a greater amount of ambivalence, for he must learn to adjust to the norms of the Street Institution, as well as try to maintain some affinity with the norms of the larger society.

THE REGULAR

The Regular is an accepted member in the Street Institution although he is not bound to all of its norms. He is the youngster who gets along with almost everyone without compromising his own value system. His ability to interact with his peers, and not be totally influenced by them, is a tribute to his uniqueness.

He is "one of the boys" and again he is not. The Regular is able to vacillate roles because he has never made a full commitment to the Street Institution. Actually his primary values are closer to white middle class values than those of his peers. He is usually a good student, conforms to most conventional laws, has close family ties and rarely belongs to a gang. Yet, despite his allegiance to white middle class norms, he knows enough about the Street Institution to function within it without undue stress. Because his coping posture is more flexible that his peers, he is able to "free enterprise" and engage in only those activities which he feels are relatively safe.

This is not to suggest that the Regular does not encounter any difficulties. The very fact that he lives in the black ghetcolony is in itself a traumatic experience. But the Regular is able to neutralize his problems with greater success and, therefore, minimize their recurrences. Of course, all Regulars do not make it past the boundaries of the ghetcolony. Most remain there despite their obedience to conventional norms. And though they may never find themselves stigmatized in the same manner as the Jester or the Antagonist, their destinies will most likely be determined by the same oppressive forces.

THE ANTAGONIST

Some boys are so lacking in coping skills that the only way for them to compensate for these deficiencies is through overt aggressive behavior. The Antagonist gains status from his ability to outfight, bully, harass and intimidate others. While it is not uncommon for ghetcolony children to exhibit volatile behavior, the Antagonist's aggression exceeds community norms. It is a role which quickly gains a boy a reputation which is both revered and feared. The Antagonist is not a leader in the classic sense, yet he is able to mobilize supporters because of his ability to overpower people. He is seen as one who has a lot of "guts" and is among the first sought after by older gang members to join their ranks.

The Antagonist is disliked by most of his peers but they will, nonetheless, cater to him because of the physical threat he poses. The administrators have labeled him as being "hard to reach," "incorrigible," and "delinquent" and have already given up on ever helping him develop his real potential. By the age of ten the Antagonist has acquired a reputation that will, undoubtedly, remain with him until his death, which in most cases, it will probably result in the kind of violence that he has expressed most of his life.

Like the other boys, his basic personality will be molded during his formative years, and because the environment in which he lives will hardly change, his behavior will remain fixed also.

Although the roles which I have briefly described vary in form, each in its own way gives a boy attention, prestige and status, all basic human needs of people. But equally important, they are reinforced by the Street Institution and, therefore, allow a boy to fit into one of the molds that helps create the lifestyles of the ghetcolony. ghetcolony.

PEER RELATIONSHIPS

Street corner groups are quite common in North Lawndale and small clusters of unsupervised boys can usually be observed hanging around alleys, taverns, pool halls or just milling on the sidewalk. The group becomes the all important influence on the black child. Few boys function independently of groups. They need to participate in groups because that is where most of their needs are met. The group offers the child a reinforcement which he does not receive at home, church, school or in the various youth serving agencies. It helps him to successfully get through the Street Institution. Though we know it is not at all unusual for children to seek companionship with their peers, black children seem to have a greater need for group attachment. This is probably due to the great amount of dependency the black child places on the group. Because other institutions have failed him, the black child is forced to seek support from his peers.

Boys also congregate in groups because they realize that groups serve as bases of power. Even at their young age they are conscious of the fact that numbers provide a deterent to the aggressive acts of others. Though pre-adolescent groups are not generally conceived as being "street gangs", members will ban together to confront another group if one of their members is intimidated. However, most boys under twelve form cliques and only engage in minor scrimmages with other cliques when they are left with no alternatives. These conflicts between cliques usually do not result into long term rivalries.

As boys grow older the cliques which they belong to either disperse or are absorbed into older aged groups. It is during this transition that belonging to a group begins to take on notoriety. Whereas the cliques were looked upon as being natural grouping of peers, the older street groups are conceived as gangs. And though the word gang is as American as cherry pie, in that it has always been a part of her tradition, the older street groups which are formed in the ghetcolony are seen as threats to this heritage. Yet they make up an essential part of the Street Institution. It's difficult for most boys to satisfactorily complete its courses without having some involvement with gangs.

The formation of gangs is inevitable. It constitutes just another one of the defense mechanisms that allows black youths to cope with oppression.

In recent years the status of the street gang has taken on a most notorious image. To many people, gangs have grown to such uncontrollable heights that few know how to deal with them. And the members of these gangs are the same pre-adolescents who just a few years earlier were beginning to familiarize themselves with the culture of the streets. They have now emerged as a "manchild" and the cycle of ghetcolony masculinity progresses one step further.

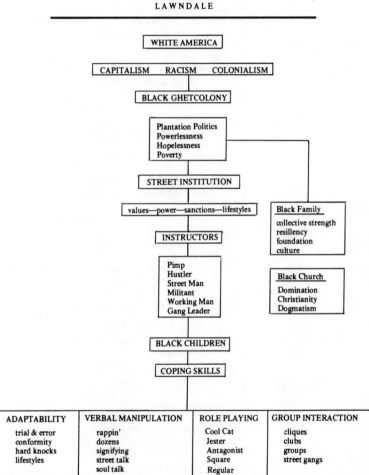

STREET INSTITUTION OF NORTH
LAWNDALE

WHITE AMERICA

CAPITALISM   RACISM   COLONIALISM

BLACK GHETCOLONY

Plantation Politics
Powerlessness
Hopelessness
Poverty

STREET INSTITUTION

values—power—sanctions—lifestyles

Black Family
collective strength
resiliency
foundation
culture

INSTRUCTORS

Pimp
Hustler
Street Man
Militant
Working Man
Gang Leader

Black Church
Domination
Christianity
Dogmatism

BLACK CHILDREN

COPING SKILLS

ADAPTABILITY	VERBAL MANIPULATION	ROLE PLAYING	GROUP INTERACTION
trial & error	rappin'	Cool Cat	cliques
conformity	dozens	Jester	clubs
hard knocks	signifying	Antagonist	groups
lifestyles	street talk	Square	street gangs
	soul talk	Regular	

BEHAVIORAL TRAITS OF BLACK GHETCOLONY
CHILDREN IN THE STREET INSTITUTION

AGES	TRAITS LEARNED
12	- is ready for street gang activities - has good awareness of street culture - becomes more clothes conscious - knows the life styles of the pimp, hustler, street man, militant, etc. - can rap with adults - may begin having sex relations - has formed an image of himself - may begin smoking reefers or dropping pills - becomes skeptical of social insitutions
11	- begins associating with older boys - begins to use the word "muthafucker" - sex interest increases - is able to distinguish youth officer, truant officer - signifies and plays the dozen consistently - spends most of his leisure time hanging around on street - may have engaged in his first misdeameanor
10	- becomes more inquisitive about sex - becomes more acquainted with weapons - learns how to rap - becomes more active with groups - begins to establish his street image - is able to see certain ambiguities in society - becomes more proficient with street language - is aware of community's "hot spots" - begins to perfect his coping skills - begins to experiment with cigarettes and sometimes alcohol and dope
9	- becomes a better fighter - learns about policy, craps, etc. - begins to identify with certain specific groups - begins occasional truancy - becomes familiar with ghetto life styles - begins to challenge authority models - realizes the need to develop "coping skills" - begins to spend more time on the streets
8	- begins to hang with small groups - begins to learn self-defense - begins to learn how to signify and play dozens - knows the meaning of "pussy" and "fuck" - has a fair understanding of his poverty - begins to develop certain inferiority feelings about race - begins to have certain negative attitudes toward his community - begins to develop poor attitude toward school

CHAPTER FOUR

THE TEENAGE ENIGMA:
THE CULTURE OF THE STREET GANG

> Negro youth are certainly no longer
> invisible, accepting their lot and
> condition in silent resignation.
> There is the ferment of change but
> not heartening change in either
> quantity or quality. From all indi-
> cations Martin Luther King's "summer
> of discontent" will be followed by
> winters and more summers of discontent,
> with youth vociferous and unrestrained
> in expression of their discontent.
>
> Lewis W. Jones
> The New World View of Negro Youth

The streets of North Lawndale are cramped with youth groups who walk arrogantly through its acres of poverty as though they were victorious soldiers occupying an alien land, yet still poised in a state of combat readiness for fear of enemy reprisal. And like conquering soldiers they feel that the spoils belong to those who are the strongest. At times these groups seem to be at odds with everyone. They become rebel fugitives in their own community and even many of the street instructors look at them with disdain. While it is a product of the Street Institution, the street gang has its own set of values which at times conflict with the cultural norms of the ghetcolony. The black street gang is truly an enigma because it challenges all authority which attempts to infringe on its sovereignty. And many of its activities only compound the crises which already exist in the black ghetcolony.

At Sixteenth Street and Pulaski Road four youths in a stolen vehicle pull alongside a curb and without provocation one of them levels a shotgun at three other youths, leaving one of them lying on the dirty pavement bleeding from shotgun pellets.

At the Marquette Street police station, two businessmen file a complaint claiming that members from a gang tried to extort money from them. However, when the desk sergeant asked them would they be willing to identify the culprits, they lower their heads and leave, apparently fearful of gang reprisal.

Near one of the Upper Grade School Centers six gang members hover at a corner and threaten younger boys who pass by if they refuse to join their ranks. One twelve year old boy refuses and is kicked in the stomach until he begins to vomit blood.

At a social agency dozens of aroused parents meet with youths and community leaders to discuss what can be done about the gangs terrorizing the streets. After four hours of futile debate, they leave still burdened with the same crisis.

At the Central Police Headquarters members of the Gang Intelligence Unit and other law enforcers discuss strategy on how to deal with gangs. Their recommendation: simply to annihilate them.

In Washington, D.C., a group of weary senators are busy writing proposals which will give them power to subpoena gang members and hold hearings concerning alleged misuse of funds by certain gangs.

If one were to view these incidents without investigating their authenticity he would, no doubt, arrive at the conclusion that black street gangs pose the most serious threat to this society since the purge of alleged communists during the McCarthy witch hunts and even more grim than the Klu Klux Klan, Nazi Party, Weathermen,

Mafia and other organized crime syndicates.

The black street gang problem is creating new law enforcement legislation, beefed up police departments, reprisals from community groups and inquiries from federal, state and local authorities. Many feel that the street gangs have gotten completely beyond control or salvation and that the only cure to their menace is to eradicate them. But how does one go about exterminating street gangs when they are the outgrowth of younger boys who graduate into their ranks after serving apprenticeship in the Street Institution? It stands to reason that this cycle cannot be severed unless we intervene in the social process that breeds gangs and makes them necessary for a youth to survive the ghetcolony. And how can this intervention be implemented when the ghetcolony offers few alternatives to youths and continues to be an oppressed community with few opportunities to enhance their social development?

"If ya don't belong to a gang the other boys will beat ya up."

"What else is dere to do when dere ain't nuthing else?"

"At least dey (the gang) make me feel like somebody."

The youths, on the other hand, claim that gangs are being unjustly persecuted and too often the positive effects they have on the community are ignored. They feel alienated from the decision-making process which governs their lives and see a need to have their own base of power to express the feelings and needs of their members. They are also critical of America's hypocrisy that makes it difficult for black ghetcolony youths to move into the broader mainstream of society.

"Man dey keep telling ya to go to school and everything will be mellow. Dat's bullshit! Dere ain't no jobs for us noways."

"Yeah if ya get busted once man...dat's it. Ain't no second chance for no nigger. Not in this fuckin' world."

And they are aware of the violence in America.

"To get somethin' outta this world man...ya have to take it. Just like them honkies did the Indians."

"Dose Mafia cats sur got it made. Dey can get away with just about anything. Dey some mean dudes."

CHICAGO STREET GANG DEVELOPMENT

Chicago has always been a breeder of street gangs. In 1927, Frederick M. Thrasher, a sociologist at the Universtiy of Chicago, completed a massive study of 1,313 Chicago street gangs. His findings revealed that street gang members came from all ethnic groups, but that the greatest percentage of them were the off-springs of immigrant families. The number of black street gangs in Chicago, at the time of this study, constituted 7.16 percent of the groups surveyed. Most of the groups mentioned by Thrasher were located in blighted areas and their members' ages ranged from ten to twenty-four years old. Also there were twenty-five gangs that had white and black members.

In making a comparison between the percentage of black street gangs and other gangs, Thrasher stated:

A comparison of the percentages of gangs of negro
race and of white foreign and native extraction
with the percentage of boys of these groups in
Chicago shows that the gang is largely a phenomenon
of the immigrant community; that the negro population of the city provides more than its share of
such groups; and that the native white population
of native percentage, which has 25.70 percent of
the boys, contributes only 5.25 percent of the gangs.[1]

During this period, the most notorious street gangs were the Irish, Italians, Poles, Jews and some Chinese groups, known as "tongs." Some of these street gangs even controlled political and business interests in their communities. In his book about Mayor Daley, entitled *Boss,* Mike Royko, a Chicago columnist, identifies one group which the mayor belonged to as being the most powerful and influential neighborhood club in Chicago, The Hamburg Social and Athletic Club was located in the community of Bridgeport, where the mayor still lives, and the reports of the Illinois Commission on Human Relations revealed that it played a dominant role in the riots of 1919. Royko also states that many prominent politicians and judges were members of this organization. But these early Chicago street gangs were not repressed in the same manner that the black street gangs are today. Instead, they were allowed to romp the street with little police intervention until their members decided to change their attitudes and become recipients of America's prosperity. Many white gang members merely ceased their gang activity when opportunities became available to them. But these options were not open to black street gang members. And when it became apparent to them that they could not achieve mobility through so-called legitimate means, many chose to remain with the gang.

The youths who live in the black ghetcolony are by far the most damaged victims of oppression. Because they are shut off from all decision-making roles which affect their lives, they seek other alternatives to compensate for this exclusion. And the most viable alternative which they can find is the street gang. For black ghetcolony youths, the gang becomes the principle defense mechanism for them to cope with the maligned conditions which are caused by oppression. Unlike most adults, youths are more impulsive and inclined to express themselves regardless of the laws which are established to regulate people. They see themselves as outsiders who must depend on their own collective strength to insure their survival. Since most institutions in the black ghetcolony fail to prepare them to cope with oppression, they develop their own means to counteract its crippling effect on their lives. But the street gang is more than a coping apparatus for black youths to express their frustrations and hostilities. For many it is the only vehicle they have to uplift themselves from the deep rooted scars of oppression.

The gang mentality syndrome even extends itself to the penal institutions. One might think that in such a suppressive environment gang members would not have the time to become involved with such things as control of turf, recruitment of new members and gang banging. But the gang problem is quite acute in most Illinois penal institutions. This is especially true at Pontiac State Prison where, at one time, gang members were allowed to openly display their allegiance to their groups, hold meetings and maintain other types of gang rituals. In fact, most gangs managed to group their members in the same cell houses: thereby re-inforcing the gang structure. The ironic thing about the extension of the gang mentality syndrome into the prison is that most gang members at Pontiac were serving time because of their gang activities. As one would suspect, rivalries, grudges and petty arguments were common occurrences among opposing gang members. As a result of these inter-group tensions, there arose many confrontations between certain gangs, the most serious one resulting in the death of two inmates in 1970. What this suggests is that the influence of the street gang is far reaching and despite the fact that gang members may be placed in confinement, the code of the gang continues to be a dominant factor in their lives.

While the gang problem in Chicago does represent a cross-section of ethnic groups, it is the black street gang which receives the greatest notoriety today. Unlike his white counterpart, the black gang member must cope with far more adversities and as a result his reaction to them are often more violent. Despite claims by law enforcement officials that all gang behavior stems from the same causes, this rationale ignores the fact that the black street gang is the product of an oppressive system which is acutely hostile to black people. The black street gang cannot be characterized by the classic terms generally used to define delinquent behavior. The labels which Clowin and Ohlin attached to street gangs, in their widely acclaimed book, *Delinquency and Opportunity,* do not typify the contemporary black street gang. Today's black street gang is neither "conflict," "retreatist" nor "fighting" oriented but a much more complex social structure that has been shaped by factors which are primarily political in nature and racist in origin. The black street gang is not just a transitional social unit for youths to give vent to their frustration and anger. It should now be realized that its expressions are more profound than simply extoling so-called anti-social behavior. When we appraise it from a historical perspective, we can see that its development stems from years of enslavement, deprivation and political oppression.

This appraisal can be substantiated by the fact that prior to being brought to America as slaves, African people were the descendants of well disciplined cultures. And even though slaves were partially cut off from their heritage, they still maintained some of their discipline when placed on the plantation, despite the punitive tactics employed by their slavemaster. But the effects of slavery eventually destroyed the orderly tradition of African people by disrupting their greatest strength, the family unit. When this occurred, African youths were left without the guidance they sorely needed to maintain harmonious relations among themselves and their communities. However, it was not until after Reconstruction, when large numbers of Blacks migrated to northern cities, that gang activity became a serious problem in the black community. Around the beginning of 1900 and especially after World War One, cities such as New York, Detroit, Philadelphia and Chicago began to feel the impact of this new development. As E. Franklin Frazier stated, "Because of the dissolution of the rural folkways and mores, the children in these families have helped to swell the ranks of juvenile delinquents." Mr. Frazier commented that the growth of delinquency among black youths in Chicago started at the turn of the twentiety century.

> The relation of juvenile delinquency to
> the organization of the Harlem Negro
> community is not so apparent as in
> Chicago, where, as we shall see, it is
> definitely related to the economic and
> cultural organization of the Negro community.

> In Chicago the percentage of Negro de-
> linquent cases among the cases brought

before the juvenile court has steadily
increased since 1900. In that year 4.7
percent of all cases of boys before the
court were Negro boys. The percentage
of Negro boys increased for each five-
year period until it reached 21.7 in 1930.[2]

But the formation of black street gangs during this period was
slight as evidenced by the following statement by the Chicago
Commission on Race Relations in a report following the violent
Chicago race riot of 1919.

Gangs whose activities figured so prominently
in the riot were all white gangs, or "athletic
clubs." Negro hoodlums do not appear to form
organized gangs so readily. Judges of the
Municipal court said that there are no gang
organizations among Negroes to compare with
those found among young whites.[3]

These comments clearly show that black youths did not have a
tradition of gang affiliation but due to the overwhelming poverty in
the black community and the increase in population this problem
became more critical.

In Chicago, black street gangs did not pose a major problem
until the advent of the 1930 Depression. In their definitive study, on
black life in Chicago during this period, St. Clair Drake and Horace
Cayton made the following observation which describes this
emergence of delinquent activity in the ghetcolony.

In 1930, 20 out of every hundred boys hailed
before the juvenile court were colored boys.
The rates for girls were almost as high.
The Depression made a chronic condition acute.
Parents were without money to give children
for the shows, the dances, and the "zoot suits"
which lower-class adolescent status required.
There were few odd jobs. Purse snatching became general in lower-class areas and even on
main thoroughfaires. Occasionally, too, a gang
of youngsters would crowd some other child who
had a little money into a doorway and rob him
at knife point. Studies of delinquents show
that their behavior is partly "rational" (e.g.
partly the search for a thrill of excitment.)[4]

Drake and Cayton called these delinquents "wild children" and though their study did not go into any analysis of the gang problem, it did touch upon the growing development of delinquency in the black communities of Chicago.

During the early 30's some violent black street gangs did begin to take form, mostly in the Black Belt on Chicago's South Side. One of the maiden groups was the Four Corners, a gang of young men, who hung around the location of 35th Street and Indiana Avenue, which was then known as the "bucket of blood."

This group started as an athletic club, but due to the high unemployment and the ensuing depression began to engage in minor felonies. The Four Corners reigned for nearly ten years until around 1940 when another large group called the Deacons emerged. The Deacons were soon augmented by other gangs such as the 13 Cats, the Destroyers and a few groups in the Maxwell Street district on Chicago's west side. The expansion of black street gangs continued during the World War II years until no black community was spared from their presence.

Unlike the well organized and often violent gangs of today, these early black street gangs engaged primarily in street fights and some misdemeanors. Members of these gangs usually sported colorful sweaters or jackets to identify their group. This custom was eventually curtailed when gang members felt that these symbols only made them more prone to police harassment. In the 60's this custom was revitalized when many gang members began to wear berets to promote their group identity.

Around 1960 North Lawndale was besieged with gangs.

Neither youth officials, police, nor social service agencies could do anything to curb this growth. Two gangs, the Egyptian Cobras and the Vice Lords, comprised the major groups. The Egyptian Cobras were located primarily west of Pulaski Road in K-Town, while the Vice Lords' territory was east of this street. During a span of 12 years there was a bitter rivalry between these groups and the streets of North Lawndale erupted with their aggressive activity. Gang wars were frequent and many youths were killed in defense of their group's reputation. Both groups appeared determined to establish themselves as the monarch of North Lawndale, and in the pursuit of this goal defied most all authority.

The culture of the gang had now become a permanent part of the black ghetcolony. It offered to many black youths, for the first time, an opportunity to gain status and recognition, something which, heretofore, they did not have. And once the precedent for gangs was established, as being an inevitable occurrence in ghetcolony life, there was no stopping their growth, nor the increased number of youths they attracted.

SOCIAL STRUCTURE OF THE BLACK STREET GANG

The social structure of the Vice Lords and the Egyptian Cobras was similar in that they both had a hierarchy of subgroups which consisted of seniors, juniors, and midgets. From these subgroups, branches or divisions were established throughout each group's turf or territory. These groups all had a common surname which showed affiliation with the major group, although they would prefix this title with a name of their own, i.e., Gestapo Cobras, Maniac Lords, etc. And within the boundaries of each group's turf, these names were sprawled on building to glorify a group's image and to serve as a deterrent to rival groups trespassing on their territory.

The social structure of these gangs was augmented by fragmentary groups and auxiliary groups, which tended to make it difficult to identify the total composition of a given group. Gang formation in North Lawndale is often spontaneous and does not always adapt to a prescribed pattern. This confusion sometimes accounts for the fact that one group may get blamed for what another groups does, because there is the lack of a definitive group structure and a consistent set of norms to govern all members. One of the problems large groups encountered in North Lawndale, when they attempted to build "youth nations," was that it became impossible to maintain control over maverick groups which insisted on keeping their autonomy, even though these groups would align themselves with the larger groups when it was convenient for them. Despite efforts to unify divergent groups, these aspiring youth nations found themselves confronted with the same organizational conflicts which have prevented other adult groups from forming functional coalitions.

Since the expansion and durability of a gang depend upon its ability to constantly recruit new members, younger boys in the Street Institution are closely screened to determine their readiness for gang membership. Because of their savvy and street knowledge, the Cool Cat, Jester and the Antagonist are always prime candidates for recruitment.

The senior members usually constitute the ruling body and are primarily responsible for seeing that the subordinate groups adhere to their policies. Mobility from one group to another is determined by age, knowledge of street culture, fighting ability and having "soul." Most gangs have no terminating age, and many adults remain active in them, because the gang still constitutes the most prestigious symbol for black manhood.

Each gang has within its social structure an elite command that consists of a president, vice-president and a war counselor. The latter role was generally assigned to a member with the most nerve (the Antagonist), for he has the dubious responsibility of leading the group during its offensive and defensive battles and negotiating treaties with war counselors from other groups. Sometimes the gang's social structure is more refined and often consists of a ruling council, official spokesmen, lieutenants and specialized units to effectuate the best possible order and control over members.

However, a problem which confronts older groups is the emergence of younger members who attempt to challenge the leadership of older members because they feel left out of the key positions and decision-making processes. Yet the older groups realize that much of their negotiable power, to influence foundations and government agencies for funds, stems from their claiming control ove the younger members.

Often younger members are coerced into committing felonious acts to re-enforce the older gang members' authority over them. Due to their size and mobility, younger boys are used as look-outs and made to break into homes and stores. A more serious exploitation of younger members takes place when older members assign them "contracts" to shoot members from rival gangs. Older members know that if arrests are made, as the result of a shooting, the younger boys would come under the jurisdiction of the Family Court, and even if found guilty their penalties would not be as severe as that given to older members. The coercion of younger members is also used as a means to test their willingness to conform to the gang's rigid controls and demands.

Discipline over members is paramount to a gang's survival. Without this control, a gang will quickly disintegrate and lose its status. Therefore, the role of the gang leader is crucial and he must, at all times, handle himself in such a way that his position as the group's patriarch goes unchallenged. Many times a truce between two rival gangs will be violated because a disenchanted member will usurp authority. This defiance is also a way for a member, who aspires to become a leader, to mobilize dissonant members behind him. However, usually truces are only meant to be short-termed agreements and seldom do they bring about a sustained peace. It is also questionable whether or not all gang members really desire to relieve inter-group tensions, for many find gang fighting to be an indispensable trademark of the street gang culture.

In 1965, while employed at the Better Boys Foundation, a social agency in North Lawndale, I made a study of street gangs in the K-town area. This study helped to pre-identify certain delinquent-prone youths who were recruited for a special developmental program, called Operation Crossroads. A summary of this study is being presented to provide the reader with a more precise description of the formation of street gangs in North Lawndale.

Names of Groups Studied

    1 - Gestapo Cobras
    2 - Village Cobras
    3 - 14th Street Cobras
    4 - Dug-Outs
    5 - Impressions
    6 - Jr. Cassanovas
    7 - Midget Cobras

HANG-OUT OF GROUPS

Although there were a few places where groups hung out, the study did not show that these places were used exclusively by only one group. There are a few locations, such as Franklin Park and the Spot Pool Hall, on 12th Street and Kedvale, which serve as a gathering place for many groups. Other hang-outs were located in or near restaurants, school playgrounds and street corners.

LOCATION OF GROUPS

These data did not pin-point where groups were actually located in terms of a particular street or intersection. At best, group locations could only be determined within a one or two block range. Contrary to the data compiled by the Commission on Youth Welfare, groups were not found at those locations designated on the gang map printed by this agency. This does not mean that these data were invalid but only substantiate the premise that groups are mobile and frequently change their locations.

AGE RANGE OF GROUP MEMBERS

The age range of group members was found to extend from 14 to 24, with the majority falling between 14 and 17. Data did not show that boys under 13 were actual participants in these groups except in the case of the Spanish Cobras, a group located north of 12th Street. However, interviews with the indigenous workers suggested that younger age groups (9-12) do exist in the K-Town area, but are developed spontaneously and their span of maturation is short lived. (Perhaps these groups should be viewed as being clusters of peer relationships, cliques, or just small groups banning together for an activity).

HISTORICAL DEVELOPMENT OF GROUPS

Most of the groups surveyed in the study reflected that they did, at one time, have some type of relationship with the Egyptian Cobras. That is to say, it appeared that these groups were an out-growth of the Cobras and through the influence of this dominant group came into existence. This succession was further encouraged by many group members having brothers or cousins belonging to the Cobras. It should be noted that although this succession showed no formal structure (in terms of the Egyptian Cobras actually fostering and developing younger groups) it did suggest that younger aged groups were perceived by the Egyptian Cobras as being under their custodianship. Generally these groups originally started as athletic teams or as a result of members hanging around on street corners.

GROUP MOBILITY

The mobility patterns of these groups were quite diversified and showed many variations. Mobility as conceived by most groups appears to be rather nebulous and apparently without a formal structure. However, groups do recognize a given territory as being more receptive for group movement. In most cases the mobility pattern parallels the territorial pattern and quite possibly both are inter-related. These groups did not travel beyond the east boundary of Pulaski Road but were rather mobile within the K-Town area.

RESIDENTIAL PATTERNS OF GROUP MEMBERS

The residential patterns of these groups showed three pronounced characteristics. One characteristic was that members resided in a smaller area within their territorial range. The second characteristic revealed that members were quite dispersed throughout the K-Town area but tended to congregate and have their activities in a much smaller area. The third characteristic showed a residential pattern which correlated with the group's territorial pattern. Within this complexity of residential patterns it can be surmised that boys do not necessarily become members of groups because of area identification but rather become affiliated with groups due to some other attraction.

TERRITORIAL CLAIMS OF GROUPS

The turf or territory of these groups was usually similar to their mobility patterns. However, the word territory appears to have more significance to groups in terms of identifying a geographical area. Groups do acknowledge certain areas as being their territory and take pride in being the most dominant and prominent group within a given area. In fact, being the proprietors of an area is one of the status satisfactions that members receive from belonging to a group. The size of the group's territory usually denotes the size and strength of a group. Many of the group's territorial patterns overlapped, especially around the Franklin Park area, which was found to be identified with five groups. The concentration of group activity in this area is rather confusing and needs to be further probed to ascertain how groups interact with each other, establish priorities, regulate activities and still maintain their identity without infringing on each other's custodianship.

AFFILIATION WITH OTHER AGENCIES

The groups in the K-Town area have no significant relationship with other agencies except Franklin Park and the Chicago Youth Centers STREETS unit. Their affiliations with these agencies were mainly due to the athletic and recreational facilities at Franklin Park and because they had a professional worker assigned to them by the Chicago Youth Centers.

AFFILIATION WITH ADULTS

These data only showed affiliations with adults who are representatives of the Franklin Park and Chicago Youth Centers. No law enforcement people were named. Some groups did indicate that they had contacts with adults who would purchase liquor, beer or wine for them.

MODES OF RECRUITMENT

Recruitment into these groups was usually on an informal basis. The major pre-requisite for group membership were: (1) to live in the area, (2) to be tough and aggressive, (3) to be accepted by other members and (4) to be recommended by a member in good standing. A few groups did indicate that they have initiations for new members.

PERCENTAGE OF DELINQUENT MEMBERS

The study was not able to sufficiently ascertain information to show the percentage of delinquent members in groups. However, most groups did indicate a high arrest rate among members.

INTERNAL ORGANIZATION OF GROUPS

The study was only able to obtain peripheral information about the internal organization of groups:

1 - Leadership — Most groups did have the following positions: President, Vice-President and War Counselor.

2 - Ranking Order - Groups generally ranked members by:
(1) knowledge of the street culture
(2) being game
(3) aggressiveness
(4) toughness

3 - Structure — Most groups held informal meetings and their membership ranged from 14 to 250 members.

NON-GANG MEMBERS

All youths in North Lawndale do not become members of a gang. Contrary to what the public is led to believe, gang members make up less than twenty percent of any one community's youth population, although this number becomes flexible when fringe members are taken into account. Nevertheless, it is a significant figure that is given greater gravity by the news media which seems to be expert in emphasizing those news items which border on sensationalism. Non-gang members do have their own social units, but these groups, i.e., social clubs and athletic teams, are seen as legitimate social structures which embrace many of society's conventional norms. Although the street gangs do not recruit every youth, each child who lives in the ghetcolony is tempted to join its ranks. Once again the black child is confronted with a problem which makes his social adjustment more difficult. If he chooses to subvert membership in the gang he must weigh the options that are left to him and still retain his status in the Street Institution. The alternative is not always easy. Since the street gang is such an integral component of the Street Institution, the non-gang member must either compromise his values or subject himself to the intimidations and threats posed by the gang. Seldom does he receive help from adults or social institutions for they either ignore his dilemma or fail to provide him with an alternative to assure him security from the gang. The non-gang member can retain his

autonomy from the street gang but only through his own
assertiveness to overcome the gang's potent influence.

Another point of clarification is that all gang members do not
become juvenile delinquents, as defined by law. Many gang
members never appear before the juvenile or boys' courts or even
commit criminal offenses. Non-gang members are equally as prone
to individual anti-social acts as are bona fide gang members. But the
stigma that is placed on the gang is automatically projected on its
members, and, therefore, all gang members are treated as if they
were law violators.

STREET WORK PROGRAMS: DEFLATED BUFFERS

The social agencies in North Lawndale, having already turned
away many gang members, finally acknowledged the fact they were
being remiss in their responsibilities. Most of these agencies had
traditional building-centered programs which were not geared to
reach gang members. Their non-creative programs would usually
repulse gang members with their rigid set of rules which failed to
take into account the social norms of the ghetcolony. Instead social
agencies continued to offer primarily recreational activities which in
no way prepared a youth to conteract the pervasive forces in the
ghetcolony that made gang membership attractive. It became
obvious to social agencies that if gang members were to be reached
and helped a new approach had to be developed.

Finally, in 1956, the YMCA of Metropolitan Chicago initiated
its Youth Gangs Program, designed to provide "detached workers"
to work with known street gangs. Armed with only a station wagon, a
modest expense account and his own human relations skills, the
street worker ventured out into the streets to intervene in a process of
gang development that had already become firmly entrenched in the
culture of the ghetcolony. At the beginning this approach was
somewhat successful in curbing certain types of delinquent activity,
mainly that of gang conflict. But even the most ablest of street
worker was not successful in reaching the older hardcore
delinquent. The worker soon learned that providing understanding
counsel was not enough but that he also had to make the worker had
gang members opportunities for achievement which the worker had
no power to produce. Earl Doty, a former executive director of
Youth Action, describes this dilemma which weakened the
effectiveness of many workers.

> For approximately 5 years following the advent
> of street work in 1956, one of a worker's basic

tools in affecting upward mobility for ghetto
youth was "a job." While this proved to be a
valuable tool, it was generally carried forth
by a "seat of the pants" approach. There was
an absence of sophistication and any clearly
refined system was lacking.

A worker was left to develop his own "bag of
resources" and expended a great deal of energy
and time in dragging youth from one employee
to another. When a job was obtained it was
usually temporary and exploitative in nature.[5]

Later a massive street worker program called STREETS
emerged when three other agencies, the Chicago Boys Clubs,
Chicago Youth Centers and Hull House Association saw the need to
coordinate their efforts. In 1967, this program was centralized under
one agency called Youth Action, which was able to expand its
services with the acquisition of federal funds. Still the problem of
gangs persisted and gang activity accelerated. Whereas gang
involvement had been seen as an inescapable stage which most
ghetcolony youths go through, the gang had now achieved greater
sophistication and it became advantageous for young adults to
remain in their ranks.

Although many street workers performed their duties with great
enthusiasm and dedication, the results of their efforts were thwarted
by the lack of cooperation from big business and other formal
institutions to open their doors to gang members. The business and
political barons of Chicago were simply concerned with pacifying the
activities of street gangs and not with providing their members with
opportunities that would enable them to escape their world of
oppression. And the street worker became the buffer agent by which
this could be accomplished. Despite the large amounts of funds
allocated to street work programs, the black street gang problem
grew to even greater proportions. Mr. Doty comments on this self
generating phenomenon.

There are unmistakable signs throughout
Chicago that what were once viewed as
young, unemployed, itinerant adults are
increasingly being viewed and labeled as
gangs by themselves and by most of society.
The resources of school, job, marriage,
jail and death no longer adequately entice

and absorb the spin-off of gang-oriented
youth.[6]

GANG INTELLIGENCE UNIT: A VIOLENT NON-SOLUTION

Police officials were also watching the growth of the black street
gang with alarm, and,in 1967,created the Police Gang Unit to deal
aggressively with the gang. A statement of recommendation to form
such a unit is extracted from the 1967 report of the Citizen's
Committee to Study Police-Community Relations:

> Finding 1.22. The Committee finds that the
> menace of youthful criminals on the streets
> of Chicago is a serious problem, both to police morale and to
> police morale and to troubled citizens.
> Police are often frustrated by having to
> "soft pedal" their treatment of youthful
> hardened criminals who commit "man-sized"
> crimes. At the same time, citizens in the
> troubled neighborhood where these youths
> roam as gangs are equally frustrated in
> their attempt to lead a law abiding life,
> to raise their families and to instruct their
> children as to the value of responsible citi-
> zenship. There is no excuse, sociologically
> or for any other reason, for failure to crack
> down on unlawful activities of these gangs,
> such as shakedowns from school children for
> their lunch money, which terrorize an entire
> community.

> We find that there is need for increased
> police activity geared solely toward the
> destruction of these gangs and the apprehen-
> sion and conviction of those gang members who
> commit crimes.[7]

That the Chicago Police Department would concur with this
recommendation only attests to its own lack of understanding
regarding the development of gangs in the ghetcolony. On March 3,
1967, a task force of five special patrol units, consisting of ten men
each, was organized to deal with the street gangs. This group was
expanded on March 21, 1967 under the leadership of Lieutenant
Edward Buckney, an outspoken critic of street gangs. The newly
formed Gang Intelligence Unit was housed in the old Chicago Park

District building at 57th and Cottage Grove in Washington Park. There the Gang Intelligence Unit (GIU) maintained up-to-date profiles on every conceivable street gang in Chicago and kept current information on the whereabouts of most gang members.

In the carrying out of its mission, the GIU seemed more disposed in using its brawn instead of its brains in dealing with street gangs. It generally had unrestricted power to carry out gestapo-like tactics in quelling their activities.

"Dey come at ya like mad animals and throw ya up against the wall for nuthin' at all," commented one indignant gang member.

A spokesman from one of the gangs in North Lawndale stated. "Dey (GIU) are out to get us. All leaders and anyone else who's suppose to be a troublemaker."

A street worker confirms these allegations.

"I try to tell them (gang members) to be cool. The GIU ain't foolin'. Man those cats don't dig me either."

The GIU justified its existence.

"We are doing what we are being paid for. Destroy the gangs. It's as simple as that."

And try they did. Within a year after the creation of the GIU, the number of gang members arrested increased considerably. However, though the GIU was persistently putting pressure on street gangs, gang wars continued, and the size of some street gangs even grew larger. Often gang members would accuse the GIU of being the perpetrators of gang wars. There were even stories of gang members being taken out of their "hoods" and placed in "hoods" of other gangs where they could be easily vamped upon, thereby futhering conflict between rival groups. And it became quite common for GIU members to disguise themselves as undercover men to infiltrate street gangs. These undercover tactics would also be used at community rallies demonstrations, meeting, social affairs and any other kind of activity which might involve youths. The GIU deemed all of its tactics justifiable, so long as they helped to curb the activities of street gangs.

No doubt there was a real need to quell the violent activities of the street gangs. Something had to be done to put an end to the senseless gang killings which were occurring almost each day in the ghetcolony. But it should have also been obvious that the tactics employed by the GIU were no remedy for the street gang problem. When youths are raised in violence, they are not intimidated by it; even when it is administered by those who are police officials. The

GIU has since been dismantled and, in 1973, the Gang Crimes Investigation Division took its place. But there is little evidence to suggest that this new unit will deviate from the unsavory tactics of its predecessor; that is until the Chicago Police Department rids itself of its own tendencies toward violence.

POLITICS AND THE BLACK STREET GANG

The war on Chicago's black street gangs was seen by some as being a move to curtail their political potential. A member of one community organization put it this way.

> The gang constitutes a major political
> power which city hall is afraid of. It
> (city hall) realizes that the youth in
> our community cannot only swing votes but
> also, and through legitimate means, begin
> to control some of the economy which has
> been controlled by white suburbia.[8]

The political potential of black street gangs first became evident during Chicago's Freedom Movement in 1964. Gang members were encouraged to participate in rallies, act as marshalls during demonstrations and take part in civil rights discussions. Leaders of the movement felt that this involvement would help it show greater strength and give gang members an opportunity to improve their civic image. But this move was not without criticism. Some people felt that the gangs were only using the movement to put them in a negotiable position with community organizations to secure jobs for members. Conversely, community organizations which used gangs were accused of exploiting gang members only as a tool to further their own bases of power. Both accusations were probably correct, but vested interests always have a priority when goals depend upon reciprocal relationships.

While there does exist a potential for greater political involvement among gang members, we should be cautious about the type of political involvement that is advocated for this fertile population. If we only define political involvement in terms of supporting existing political parties then I have strong reservations about its long-term value. Influencing youths to merely re-enforce those political structures that have historically contributed to the oppression of black people is counter to any people who are struggling to control their lives. Unless we are advocating a broader political involvement, one that incorporates ways and means to gain total liberation, then we are only contributing to our own destruction. Political involvement for black youths must teach them to challenge every level of this country's political economic structure. They must not be fed with illusions of achieving political parity but must be indoctrinated to revolutionary ideologies which can prepare them to take full command of their destinies. At present the solution to the black man's oppression in this country does not lie in the paternalistic programs of either major political party. Organizations which hold to this belief are only perpetuating the myth of American democracy and mis-directing black youths to channel their energies in a direction that ignores the racial pathology that is so entrenched in the institutional fabric of American life.

At one time, the Black Panther Party was making some efforts to politicize street gangs to become involved in constructive community activities. However, this was during the period when the Black Panther Party was engaged in constant confrontations with the police and its own image was being challenged as a subversive and violent organization. Also, many street gangs resisted these efforts because they felt that the Black Panther Party was infringing on their territories and would divert members from their groups. When the climate for an allegiance between street gangs and the Black Panther Party became favorable, the police had clamped down so hard on these groups that a coalition was not possible. Some people felt that the police realized the potential of such a coalition and made every effort to abort its formation.

Although the Chicago Freedom Movement did not achieve its goals, the power of the gangs had risen considerably. Gang leaders began to realize that their members composed a large majority of the ghetcolony and believed that if any community organization was to represent the people, it must have the support of the gangs to legitimize its claim. The same was true of public, state and government sponsored agencies which were starting youth programs in the ghetcolony. For them to function, they, too, needed to involve gang members. Because of this need, public, private and community organizations began to struggle for gang representation. This struggle found some agencies trying to induce gang members with all sorts of promises, and consequently some members found themselves on the payrolls of more than one agency. It seemed that all at once everyone wanted to do something for the gangs, but this was only because the gangs could be fronted off, exploited and manipulated for political motivations. But gang leaders were not naive to what was going on and, as agencies solicited their support, they began to place greater demands on the agencies. Some gangs became so sophisticated that they formed their own non-for-profit corporation (apparently with the assistance of white "liberals") and began writing proposals for funds to implement their own programs. And as always funds were allocated on the basis of how much power a group had in the ghetcolony.

Since community power is basically a reflection of numbers, gangs began to increase their ranks. Procurement of new members became a top priority and, in their recruitment, gangs began to expand their territories. The expansion of "hood" ultimately encroached upon the hoods of other gangs and, as a result, major gang wars ensued. Unlike earlier gang rumbles, which were generally fought over the intrusion of territory and petty differences, the gang wars were now being waged over expanded boundaries and increased membership which were the main indicators of a group's power to attract funds. Some gangs magnified their ranks by forming alliances with other groups and the size of a few took on astronomical proportions. But the price for maintaining large groups was costly and many youths became victims in the struggle to build youth nations. Fratricide among black gangs was rampant.

Hardly a day went by without some youth being shot or beaten.

The street warriors were no longer seen as restless soldiers just o occupying a land but as mercenaries who were determined to govern their hoods, at any cost.

But the police were not to be threatened by this new wave of gang activity, and began to counteract this aggression through increased police retaliation. As usual black gang members had no one to turn to who they could trust. Few adults, social agencies or community organizations in the ghetcolony were willing to assume any responsibility for neutralizing the problem. One of the reasons there exist strained relations between the black street gang and the black community is the lack of trust each has of the other. The black community often shows little faith in its own youth. And, on the other hand, many black youths have lost their confidence in the black community. This lack of trust in each other was clearly shown during the turbulent days of the first Chicago Plan, a program that was supposedly designed to get more jobs for members of minority groups in the building and trade unions. Under the leadership of the Coalition for United Community Action, black youth gangs helped stop work at many construction sites to dramatize the racist policies of the building and trade unions. Without their support, the CUCA would have had little leverage in dealing with the awesome power of organized labor. But after a series of fiascos, violent demonstrations and political sabotage, the

Chicago Plan faltered, without making any significant impact on the labor market. Afterward, many gang members were arrested, and the black community failed to mobilize any real support to help them; when it was obvious some had been apprehended for political reasons.

Gang leaders began to claim foul! They accused community organizations of using them only when it served their interest. But when things got tough, these groups abandoned them for their own survival. While these allegations have never been fully substantiated, it is true that the size and strength of many street gangs began to decrease after the Chicago Plan failed.

Distrust between street gangs and community organizations continued, and neither group appeared willing to improve their tensed relationships. Instead, some community organizations began to join the "law and order" chorus, and to assist the police in its crackdown of street gangs. Finally some street gang leaders realized the futility of such a relationship and wrote a joint manifesto with the Illinois Black Panther Party, as an appeal for solidarity in the black community.

A MANIFESTO FROM THE TEEN NATIONS AND BLACK PANTHER PARTY

Addressed to Fathers, Sons, Brothers, Mothers, Daughters and Sisters in the Black Community

Basic contentions now exist in the Black community which we want to help settle. Teen nations do not think of themselves as inimical to the best interest of this community.

We therefore go on record as being opposed to all violence in the Black community. Violence is the matrix of which we developed individually as men and collectively as teen nations. All of us must bear our share of responsibility for it. In our desire to grow to the stature of full manhood, we are willing to take responsibility both for what we have done to our brothers and what we have failed to do.

On the other hand, permit us to say, for the record, that we are not responsible for all the violence in the Black community. Much of it has been visited upon us from the outside, and likewise we are victims of the most damnable and systemic violence ever committed upon a people. The reason such violence exists is that all of us have failed to understand clearly what our goals ought to be as well as failed in developing tools, techniques, know-how and images for reaching these goals. Again, we have not developed an ethic or etiquette, which says that we are responsible to and accountable for one another, and which delineates the ways in which such responsibility and accountability work.

The important thing is that fathers, sons and brothers must live and work more intimately and effectively together. Our mothers, daughters and sisters demand this of us. Because our credibility is most in question, we pledge to take an initiative and demonstrate to the Black community that sons can be good sons, relate to others of our generation as brothers and love and respect our fathers.[9]

Although many people may question the sincerity and intent of such a magnanimous statement, the words it contain do reflect the types of relationships which must evolve if there is ever to be harmony between the street gang and the black community.

In 1968, a last ditch effort was made to rehabilitate black street gangs. Funds from private foundations and government agencies began to trickle into the hands of a few street gang organizations. Previously these funds had been given to community organizations who, in turn, were supposed to turn them into viable programs to help street gangs secure jobs for their members. But when this arrangement failed to achieve its goal, gang members were then asked to participate along with these organizations to develop more productive programs. One of these programs was Operation Bootstrap which was designed to create economic opportunities for street gangs. The history of Operation Bootstrap was a short and unsuccessful one. The reasons for its failure were many, and during its brief existence charges of mismanagement of funds, unfulfilled promises, political patronage and plain fraud were echoed by both the street gangs and participating agencies. As one gang member put it, "They gave us a strap, but not a boot for it to go on."

In North Lawndale, the Cobras received some assistance in setting up a gasoline station and car wash service. But this undertaking was shortlived. Due to improper facilities, insufficient funds, and the lack of proper management, the business lasted less than six months. Later, the Cobras managed a paper factory which was far more successful. But this venture ended in disaster when the building which housed it burned down as the result of a fire which some people believed was the work of an arsonist.

The Vice Lords, who now prefixed their name with Conservative, had a somewhat better track record. At one time, this group operated a Teen Town restaurant, a security guard service, a pool hall, two ice cream parlors, a social canteen and a shop called the African Lion. However, all of these businesses have since collasped and, today, only their relics remain.

What really happened to the small business ventures of the few street gangs which had begun to achieve some economic stability? First, I would suspect that they lacked sufficient on-going funds to have any long term success. Second, that they lacked sincere professional guidance which could have helped to manage them better. And third, the internal struggle for power between gang members coupled with the gang mentality negated the few chances these groups had to achieve even a small degree of economic security.

The failure of these paternalistic business ventures helped to contribute to the demise of large youth nations in North Lawndale. Without an economic base which could produce jobs for their members, youth nations began to lose their status as well as their power to attract new members. Though street gangs are still quite prominent in North Lawndale, they tend to be much smaller and less of a threat to the political-economic interest of the white power structure. Most of the original members of the Egyptian Cobras and the Conservative Vice Lords are either in prison, strung out on drugs, or trying to regain their reputations in the Street Institution. Of course, a few have left the Street Institution and have managed to survive without the support of the gang. But the vast proportion of older gang members in North Lawndale have yet to escape from the Street Institution, and the chances of them ever doing so are as unlikely as a blind jockey riding a one-legged horse to victory in the Kentucky Derby.

The present day gang situation in North Lawndale has not changed much. Youth groups still run rampant in the streets and younger aged boys are still coerced to join their ranks. There are periodic shoot-outs between rival gangs and even with police, which usually leave one youth maimed or killed each week. Attacks against women and older men make walking the streets after dark a macabre experience. Older gang members who have attempted to organize legitimate businesses claim to be making efforts to curb the violent aspect of the gang. Yet younger aged members still accuse the older members of fronting them off and keeping all the money. Community organizations which are trying to show a strong power base still look for the support of certain gang members, and a few social agencies are continuing their feeble efforts to neutralize gang conflict situations. Black militant spokesmen are still raving about how gangs are being persecuted, but fail to come up with any viable programs to counteract the real threats gangs pose to the community.

In recent years, some black street gangs have been accused of monitoring the drug traffic which plagues so many black ghetcolonies. This accusation has been made because many people feel that the drug traffic could not exist in the ghetcolony without street gang support or approval. Because the street gang is such a dominant force in the ghetcolony, this suspicion probably has some grain of truth. However, one should be careful in re-enforcing such an allegation until more concrete evidence is uncovered. Then, too, if street gangs are involved in drug traffic, it is quite likely that the culprits are older members who continue to use the street gang as a screen for such felonious activities.

Yet, there is a resolve among community people to deal with the gang problem. Some fear for their lives if they try to intervene in the gang's activities, while others have just given up, accepting the gang's presence as being immutable. To a great extent this feeling of hoplessness is real. North Lawndale, itself, has changed very little. it still remains in a state of inertia, perpetuating its own blight and suffering from the same chain of oppression which originally turned it into a colony. Can we really expect the gangs to diminish under these conditions?

To understand the behavior of black street gang members, it is necessary to examine the source of their attitudes. If members of gangs become hustlers, pimps, street men and other negative types, then they were definitely not born with the traits which are identified with these models. Most behavior is learned and, therefore, we must make an honest assessment of the situations and adult models from which black youths form their attitudes. Although some of the instructors in North Lawndale leave much to be desired, they have been able to develop survival lifestyles and in the ghetcolony surviving is what actually counts. Even though their lifestyles are often self-defeating and self-destructing, they become the models which are transmitted and emulated by black youths. For gang members to become positive male prototypes they must be exposed to positive adult models. In the black ghetcolony part of the problem is the adults whose lifestyles offer few alternatives for black youths.

Black ghetcolony children become black ghetcolony men because they emulate black ghetcolony lifestyles. It's time we take a look behind the scene of this never-ending cycle.

STRUCTURE OF THE BLACK STREET GANG

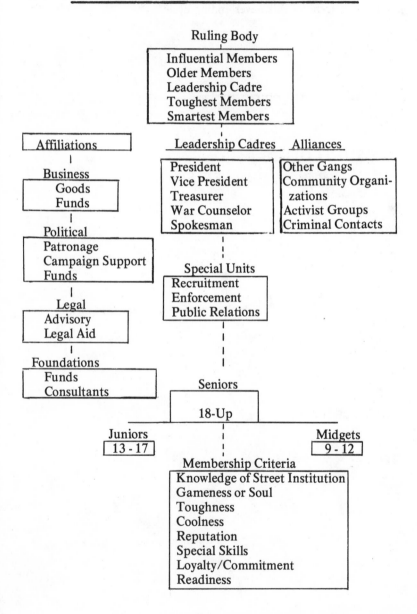

Ruling Body

| Influential Members |
| Older Members |
| Leadership Cadre |
| Toughest Members |
| Smartest Members |

Affiliations

Leadership Cadres   Alliances

Business
Goods
Funds

President
Vice President
Treasurer
War Counselor
Spokesman

Other Gangs
Community Organi-
  zations
Activist Groups
Criminal Contacts

Political
Patronage
Campaign Support
Funds

Legal
Advisory
Legal Aid

Special Units
Recruitment
Enforcement
Public Relations

Foundations
Funds
Consultants

Seniors

18-Up

Juniors
13 - 17

Midgets
9 - 12

Membership Criteria
Knowledge of Street Institution
Gameness or Soul
Toughness
Coolness
Reputation
Special Skills
Loyalty/Commitment
Readiness

CHAPTER FIVE

GHETCOLONY LIFE STYLES: FEW ALTERNATIVES

> It is very difficult, if not impossible, to understand the lifestyles of black people using traditional theories developed by white psychologists to explain white people. Moreover, when these traditional theories are applied to the lives of black folks many incorrect, weakness-dominated and inferiority oriented conclusions come about.
>
> Dr. Joseph White
> Toward a Black Psychology

It was Friday afternoon.

School was out and the streets of North Lawndale quickly filled with restless children who would now extend their education to the Street Institution, and begin to study a much more serious course—learning how to survive.

Johnny Brown, his youthful black face glittering with excitment, began to stroll along Pulaski Road after leaving some of his buddies in the school yard playing softball.

As he approached the corner of 16th Street, he stopped for a minute to observe two men sharing a bottle of wine. They looked at him with lurid eyes and teased his curiosity by shaking the bottle at him. After the gesture of temptation, Johnny continued northward until he could no longer hear their caustic laughter.

In the middle of the block a late model sedan pulled over to the curb and a large well dressed man alighted and proceeded to talk hastily to another man, who was standing nervously near a storefront church. The two men exchanged words and the driver reached into his pocket and handed the other man a small brown envelope. After receiving what appeared to be a roll of bills, the driver departed, accelerating his vehicle to a high rate of speed.

By the time Johnny reached 15th Street he had also observed two other men engaging in a violent argument, and one old man seated on a log mumbling to himself. At the corner of 15th Street, he was greeted by three of his friends, who had gathered around a tall man dressed in khaki clothes, passing out leaflets and orating about poor community conditions.

The men whom I've briefly described are a few of the instructors who serve as models in the Street Institution. They are the persons who the children of the ghetcolony become acquainted with and begin to emulate. These men are products of the ghetcolony and as such personify the values and lifestyles which are transferred to the youths. The social dynamics of any community are best reflected by the people who live there. On the other hand, the administrators of the ghetcolony, social workers, policemen, teachers and businessmen, represent only transient symbols of authority and have little influence on the intrinsic cultural patterns of the community.

No two persons are identical despite the fact they may share similar experiences and live in the same environment. Yet there are lifestyles that tend to act as a barometers for certain types of cultural behavior, and it is these lifestyles which people make a selection from and adopt as their own. Lifestyles do not develop from a vacuum. Their patterns are formed by traditions and cultural experiences which reflect the development of a particular group. When a group remains static, as in the case of most black people, then the lifestyles of its people go unchanged. The choices given to black ghetcolony children are often narrowed to self-defeating and self-destructing models whose lifestyles only reflect the hopelessness and powerlessness that accompanies restricted mobility. To help us better understand the social dynamics inherent in these models, it will be necessary to take a closer look at them.

THE FORMATION OF BLACK LIFESTYLES

To appreciate the nature of black lifestyles, we must first understand that they have emerged from an environment which is atypical. This is to say that the black ghetcolony, because of its historical development, has been shaped by forces which were designed to create coping modes of behavior. As victims of a ruthless slave system, black people have had to develop unique coping postures to adapt to an environment that was insensitive to their survival. The environment that white America created for black people was predicated on fear, frustration, anxiety and death. It was an environment which disclaimed the humanity of people, and then attempted to make these same people dependent upon the inhumanity of their oppressor. And in such a dehumanizing environment, those who are its victims take out their frustrations and anxieties on members of their own group. While this is taking place, the controllers of the oppressed environment begin to point an accusing finger at the oppressed, as being responsible for their own conditions. To justify this claim, the oppressor develops various sociological theories to re-enforce his position. Studies are fabricated, surveys grossly distorted, and social research becomes an instrument to classify the oppressed into pathological categories. This malignment of the oppressed is then used as an excuse to exercise various social experiments which are supposed to correct the so-called pathology of oppressed people. And the most disturbing thing about this "scapegoating" is that the oppressed people begin to believe the things which they are accused of being. As a result, many members of the oppressed group begin to act out the roles which the oppressor has prescribed for them.

To a large extent, the lifestyles of oppressed people have been created by the system which oppressed them. Consequently, the oppressed begin to define themselves in terms that are not conducive to their achieving a sense of self-worth. The revolutionary Brazilian prophet, Paulo Freire, provides a good analysis of this form of dehumanization.

> The oppressed, who have been shaped by the
> death-affirming climate of oppression, must
> find through their struggle the way to life-
> affirming humanization, which does not lie
> simply in having more to eat (although, it
> does involve having more to eat and cannot
> fail to include this aspect). The oppressed
> have been destroyed precisely because their
> situation has reduced them to things. In
> order to regain their humanity they must cease
> to be things and fight as men. This is a radi-
> cal requirement. They cannot enter the strug-
> gle as objects in order later to become men.[1]

And it is from this dehumanizing system that many black
people have had to develop lifestyles which, although helping them
to survive, have done little to liberate them from oppression. A study
by the Harlem Youth Opportunities Unlimited, Inc., made the
following critical analysis about this aspect of the black community.

> The psychological dimensions of the ghetto
> clearly related to, determined and re-enforced
> by objective characteristics, involve patterns
> of general hostility, random aggressiveness,
> despair, apathy, a curious fluctuation between
> self-deprecation and compensatory grandiosity
> and posturing.[2]

In North Lawndale, one can witness, almost any day the
myriad of lifestyles which black men have adopted to cope with their
oppression. The most prominent of these lifestyles can be identified
by the (1) Street Man, (2) Hustler, (3) Pimp, (4) Working Man and (5)
Militant.

STREET MAN

Bigger Thomas, the anti-hero of Richard Wright's *Native Son*,
is a classic example of the Street Man. In his absorbing and
provocative novel about a black man whose violent lifestyle is shaped
from the slums of Chicago, Wright poignantly describes how the
"nigger mentality" expresses itself through the person of Bigger
Thomas. Although Bigger is not a prototype of the black ghetcolony
man, he does represent a conglomerate of types which have become
victims of their own inner hate and the manacles of white
oppression. In discussing how Bigger was created, Wright has said.

As my mind extended in this general and
abstract manner, it was fed with even
more vivid and concrete examples of the
lives of Bigger Thomas. The urban environment of Chicago, affording a more
stimulating life, made the Negro Bigger
Thomases react more violent than even
in the South. More than ever I began to
see and understand the environmental
factors which made for this extreme
conduct.[3]

As a child in Mississippi, Wright observed different types of
Bigger Thomases and classified them as the bully, the hard nose, the
bad nigger, the rebel and the cantankerous nigger. In the ghetcolony
you can see variations of each, for they are the men who stand
around on corners, linger in taverns and display their aggressiveness
wherever they please.

The Street Man not only projects his aggression on whites but
also against members of his own group. He is inconsiderate of others
and often his anger is directed toward himself as well. He takes pride
in being able to take care of himself and feels that no challenge is too
great if it involves a physical contest. He refuses to adhere to
conventional norms, and is constantly at odds with his peers or any
other group which trespasses on his uninhibitiveness.

The Street Man is neither a leader nor follower for his behavior
vacillates according to what best serves his own interest. He realizes
he is not liked but shows no remorse because his survival does not
depend upon mutual friendships but his ability to take care of
himself in threatening situations. Despite his fierceness, he is the
most harassed and intimidated of all black ghetcolony men. When
things go down in the ghetcolony, the Street Man is the first to be
"busted." Yet his steadfast stubborness refuses to yield to
condemnation.

"I don't take shit from nobody."

"When ya fuck with me...ya better kno what cha doing."

While the Street Man is conscious of his oppression, he is
unable to deal with its manifestions. He then allows his emotions to
react against his own community. The Street Man lacks the poise of
the Hustler and sophistication of the Pimp; but he has a type of
ruggedness that is sorely needed to withstand the social oppression
of the ghetcolony.

THE HUSTLER

The Hustler is, perhaps, the most celebrated of all ghetcolony models. He has this distinction because of his uncanny ability to manipulate the ghetcolony to best serve his interest. The Hustler is a connosieur of ghetcolony culture who has learned it so well that he becomes its most prolific statesman. The Hustler possesses a variety of coping skills which makes it possible for him to reap a harvest from things that appear non-productive to others. It has been said that a good hustler can squeeze money from a turnip.

It would take a book to describe all the types of hustlers in the ghetcolony. However, two major types stand out. The first type is more criminally inclined and his activities range from pushing dope, selling policy, taking bets and sometimes soliciting prostitutes. However, the criminally inclined hustler usually will not participate in certain felonies such as armed robbery or burglary, even though he may be a middle man in the transaction of stolen goods. Still, despite this ingenuity and precautionary safeguards, the average hustler, who is criminally inclined, will eventually end up with long term confinements in jail.

The other major type of hustler is less prone to committing felonies, though he will during desperate times venture out into these more serious crimes. But his specialties are playing pool, shooting craps, conning people, exploiting businesses, making shady deals and engaging in other precarious activities which help provide him with a grubstake to survive another day.

This type of hustler is usually adept with words and has mastered the street vernacular of the ghetcolony. Many youths who develop the ability to "rap well" become good hustlers. Hustling usually demands a keen mind that is perceptive enough to exploit even the most minute of situations. The Hustler is like a parasite and will leech onto anything he can if it offers benefits. And he is also a thoughtless person who doesn't care who he hurts or the consequences of his actions.

Unlike the Street Man, the Hustler avoids physical confrontations whenever possible, for his strength lies in his ability to maneuver situations in his favor. Most hustlers like to dress well and are generally boastful about their ability to "out deal" others. At times, the Hustler will hold a steady job and adhere to some of the Working Man's virtues. But when the opportunity arises his maverick tendencies motivate him to hustling again.

The lifestyle of the Hustler is very functional in the ghetcolony because it enables a person to, seemingly, acquire things which otherwise appear unobtainable to him. Then too, it compliments the "hustling nature" of this society whose system of rewards is governed by manipulative skills. To some degree everyone in the ghetcolony possesses hustling skills, but it is the full time hustler who makes hustling a highly challenging and competitive profession.

Children admire the Hustler more than the Street Man. They see in his lifestyle a way for them to get by in this society without breaking one's back or being violent. A common remark made by black youths, when given an opportunity to work in a government financed work program is:

"Shit man. Dey expect me to waste my ass
for dat jive piece of bread. Man I can
make twice dat much out dere on the streets."

Often they are correct because the streets of the ghetcolony, as poverty stricken as they look, do have avenues for making money that are easier and pay more than $1.60 per hour job offered by most unimaginative federal programs that are aimed at providing better job opportunities for ghetcolony youths.

A ghetcolony child learns how to hustle at an early age. The more skillful hustler is the one who has observed throughout his development everything he could in the Street Institution and then is able to put these teachings into practice. The ghetcolony child who has not mastered any of the skills of hustling is destined for a much more difficult time than one who has.

THE PIMP

The most over-glamorized of all black ghetcolony men is the Pimp. The Pimp is often regarded as the "Prince of the Ghetcolony" because of the flamboyant lifestyle which he is able to maintain by exploiting women. For some black men, pimping has become an expeditious way for them to purchase fancy clothes, buy new cars and look "pretty." Pimping is by no means confined to the ghetcolony, though it is considered to be more common here than in other communities.

In the ghetcolony there are two kinds of Pimps, the Street Pimp and the Professional Pimp. The Street Pimp deals mainly with petty hustling and does not depend upon just the exploitation of women to maintain his lifestyle. Like the Hustler, he is involved in many kinds of hustling activities. Most Pimps in the ghetcolony are of this type. However, the Professional Pimp maintains his lifestyle entirely on his ability to exploit women. Unlike the Street Pimp, he does not hang around in the streets but usually lives away from the

ghetcolony in more regal surroundings. Still he will frequent the
ghetcolony on occasion to show off his wares and to impress the guys
on the corner. The Professional Pimp is thoughtless, for pimping to
him is a full-time occupation which respects no one. The life of a
Professional Pimp leads him to make deals with almost everyone in
the ghetcolony, from the Hustler, dope pusher, and juice man to
other criminal types. His lifestyle crosses each because the Pimp
must negotiate with many people to keep his profession in tact. One
of the most revealing accounts of a pimp is told by an ex-pimp called
Iceberg Slim. In his autobiographical novel, titled, *Pimp, The Story
of My Life*, Iceberg Slim tells about the tragic and horrendous
experiences which he encountered as a pimp.

> I had spent more than half a lifetime in a
> worthless, dangerous profession. If I had
> stayed in school in eight years of study I
> could have been an M.D. or a lawyer. Now
> here I was, slick but not smart, in a cell,
> I was past forty with counterfeit glory in
> my past, and no marketable training, no
> future. I had been a bigger sucker than a
> square mark. All he loses is scratch. I
> had joined a club that suckered me
> behind bars five times.[4]

Despite the glamorous image the Pimp tries to convey, his life is
far from being colorful. Instead, it is a constant struggle to outwit his
women and to keep one step ahead of the police and the enemies
who are out to destroy him. But most youths only see the glamorous
facade of the Pimp and, therefore, find his lifestyle exciting and
rewarding. Teenagers in the ghetcolony pride themselves on
making it with a chick and though they are only operating at a
superficial level, being able to make girls and have them do things
for you is a testimony to one's masculinity and coolness. In actuality
these youths who admire the Pimp are really engaging in fantasy.
Because the Professional Pimp rarely lives in the ghetcolony, youths
tend to acquaint his lifestyle with what they see in the movies or
other media. And these sources usually over-glamorize the
Professional Pimp as though he lives a life of uninhibited royalty.

   But the life of a Pimp is erratic, and his fortunes disappear as
soon as they are obtained. He is continuously manipulating everyone
and cannot afford to become lax, or his empire will collapse.
Pimping is a dangerous business and those who adopt this style of
life usually crumble before they can see its real hazards. Even the
most ardent student of the Street Institution never fully learns the

lifestyle of a pimp until he becomes one. And then it is too late. As a model, the Pimp offers black youths very little that is positive. Instead his flamboyant lifestyle only encourages them to exploit women and dissipates their chances for becoming real men.

THE WORKING MAN

All ghetcolony men do not become street men, hustlers, pimps or criminals. Most, in fact, are average working people who are trying to make it through legitimate endeavors. While they do relate to the Street Institution, it is only on a peripheral level, for the norms they try to follow come from the larger society.

The Working Man in the black ghetcolony is much like the Working Man in any other community, except he is confronted by the ever present shadow of racial oppression. But the Working Man feels he can overcome his oppression by diligent work, adherence to laws and being a "decent citizen." Of course, he carries with him a great amount of frustration, for no matter how hard he tries, it appears that he is making little progress. Still he is willing to "wait for better things to come" and will sublimate his frustration instead of violating prescribed norms to improve his status.

Although the Working Man belongs to the largest adult group in the ghetcolony, his influence is not felt as great as the Hustler, Pimp or Street Man. The reason for this is that the Working Man, after laboring all day, comes home and watches television, does odd jobs around the house and engages in other conventional chores. He does not spend as much time in the streets as other ghetcolony men. Of course he may frequent a tavern for a short beer or two and visit a pool hall on occasions, but he is not seen as a "street man" and it is in the streets where the greatest influences are projected. Consequently, he does not become a primary model for black youth. His major influence is in the home, but most ghetcolony children, unless under rigid parental control, find the streets their primary place of reference. Another factor which negates his influence over youths is that his values, being conventional oriented, do not lend themselves to counteracting the pervasive norms of the Street Institution.

Instead the Working Man is conservative in nature and avoids taking aggressive measures in dealing with his oppression. Even in his discontent he retains faith in the very system that is oppressing him. While the Working Man possesses many virtues, these attributes do not combat the adversities in the ghetcolony. There is little room for fair play in the ghetcolony and those who adhere to the golden rule are also destined to be betrayed by it. Only under the most adverse circumstances does the Working Man lower his "die-of the road" shield to participate in programs aimed at improving community conditions. He disapproves of the other ghetcolony models but lacks the incentive or power to change them. Yet he is often treated as if he were a criminal because the police make few distinctions among ghetcolony men. And though he works industriously to remove himself from the ghetcolony, he finds that his future remains imprisoned within its borders.

If the Working Man would ever overcome the mesmerizing effect the American Dream has on him, he could be a viable model to black youths. But in reality the American Dream is a nightmare in the ghetcolony and only those who are not harnessed to its myth will ever overcome their oppression. Nevertheless, the Working Man ignores this reality and continues to live a conventional life even though it does little to help him receive the benefits awarded to other law abiding citizens.

THE MILITANT

One of the questions most frequently asked after the 1966 urban riots was whether or not those who took part in them were criminally oriented persons who merely exploited a vulnerable situation or politically conscious militants who have given up on reform and saw violence as their only means to escape oppression. In one riot study this explanation was given.

> From the evidence of the riots that have
> taken place in the racial ghettos of
> large cities, a profile of the partici-
> pants may be drawn. The rioter for the
> most part was a black teenager or young
> adult between the ages of fifteen and
> twenty-four. He lived in the city in
> which he rioted. He was a high school
> dropout, usually unemployed or employed
> in menial jobs, that is, unskilled or
> service jobs. He was male and extremely
> hostile to whites, as well as to middle
> class blacks.[5]

Still another critic of these disorders, Dr. Charles V. Hamilton made this interpretation.

> We cannot term these events riots pre-
> cisely because in the minds of the

people breaking the windows and burning
the property, that authority is not duly
constituted. They are, in fact, revolts.
By this we mean that they are acts which
deny the very legitimacy of the system
itself. The entire value structure which
supports property rights over human rights,
which sanctions the intolerable conditions
in which the black people have been forced
to live is questioned.[6]

Regardless of what point of view one supported, it became
crystal clear that a new kind of black man was emerging from the
ghetcolony. Though he is called many names: rebel, renegade,
activist—his attitude and behavior are unquestionably anti-establishment. The lifestyle of the Militant is not entirely unique for it
does incorporate some of the characteristics of other ghetcolony
models. But he is imbued with a deep conviction to be liberated
which makes him stand out from the rest. The Militant refuses to be
emasculated by oppression and is determined to assert his new
found sense of strength to contest it. He possesses a keen awareness
of the political system which oppresses black people and becomes a
social advocate. His greatest assets are his ability to politicize and
mobilize people to understand that they are being victimized by both
white racism and their own subservient attitudes. Far from being a
Puritan, the Militant does, however, try to influence the Pimp, and
Street Man from further exploiting the ghetcolony. He sees these
models as detrimental to black liberation and knows that those who
emulate them are only assisting the real enemy.

The hustlers, pimps and street men generally do not care for the
Militant. First, they feel he is encroaching on their activities by
drawing people away from them. Second, that the Militant only
attracts greater police surveillance. But the youths tend to admire
the Militant because they see him as being someone with nerves and
guts to stand up against the establishment. They are also impressed
with his ethnic pride which reflects the consciousness of the black
liberation movement. Today's black ghetcolony youths have been
somewhat influenced by the emergence of black awareness and do,
in their own way, try to incorporate this new image in their own
lifestyles.

The Militant is a much needed model in the black ghetcolony.
His presence fills a void that has existed for too long; a strong
positive black male who is dedicated to raising the level of his

people. He is needed, too, not only because of his aggressiveness, (the hustler, pimp and street niggers are also aggressive) but because his aggression is aimed at alleviating oppression and not toward the maintenance of it. But all militants do not necessarily serve in the best interest of black youths. Some are only self-styled demigods whose advocacy sometimes leads youths to acts of violence which border on suicide. Those militants who only encourage youths to "take to the gun" without giving them support and a reasonable chance to survive are only exploiting the eagerness of youth to escape their plight, regardless of the circumstances. Black youths are already being victimized by white oppression and need not be conjured by black fanticism. However, as the mood of the black ghetcolony becomes more politically conscious, the number of militants will also rise. For when ghetcolony youths learn that hustling, pimping and street fighting do not, in the long term, free them from oppression, they will inevitably turn to a style of life which, historically, has been the only way oppressed people have ever gained freedom: and that is by organized resistance.

There do exist other ghetcolony models who have some influence on black children. The dope addict, alcoholic and the derelict are also instructors in the Street Institution. But these models have little influence on black youths because their behavior patterns offer them few chances for survival. Then, too, these are not really styles of life but rather the expressions of defense mechanisms which result from people being unable to satisfactorily cope with certain frustrations and anxieties which may or may not be caused by oppression. Anyone can become victimized by these expressions, regardless of his lifestyle or economic status.

What makes most ghetcolony models so distressing is that they are self-defeating and self-destructive in nature. When black youths begin to emulate these lifestyles, regardless of their survival skills, they too become self-defeating and self-destructive. And it is these traits which make it impossible for black children to rise above their lowly life status. For some models, the Pimp, the Hustler, and the Street Man, change becomes a laborious but not impossible task. Malcolm X showed us all that a man can transform himself to a new kind of black man. Malcolm X experienced every conceivable facet of ghetcolony life and yet was able to overcome it.

> I believe that it would be almost impossi-
> ble to find anywhere in America a black
> man who has lived further down in the mud
> of human society than I have; or a black

man who has been any more ignorant than I
have been; or a black man who has suffered
more anguish during his life than I have.
But it is only after the deepest darkness
that the greatest light can come; it is
only after extreme grief that the greatest
joy can come; it is only after slavery and
prison that the sweetest appreciation of
freedoms can come.[7]

But it is asking too much for everyone to be like Malcolm X.
He was an exceptionally rare individual who may never again be
equalled. Yet, the legacy of Malcolm X has influenced many black
youths and today there are more black men who are trying to
emulate the things he stood for. While this number is comparatively
small, it does provide black youths with something more
encouraging than the disillusioned models they have been
accustomed to.

MEDIA AND BLACK IMAGES

Other styles of life which make some impression on black
youths come from the television and movie media. But these models
are even more disheartening in that they only project traditional
stereotypes or unbelievable super-type black men. The current
commercial fad of showcasing a few black people on television has
done little to give black children a realistic image of their
experiences. The television media has only come up with stock
characterization of the Amos and Andy genre which rekindles racist
concepts or non-racial type black people to show that universality is
void of ethnic distinctions. In an essay on minority programming in
television, R. Arnold Gibbons makes the following appraisal of this
trend.

It is clear to see why this is so. Television must be seen as an agent of the
System which supports the underlying
philosophy of that system. It is a conspicuous purveyor of that System which
disseminates that opinion of that System.
And to avoid social crises or to meet it
only on its own terms, or when compelled
to do so, is one of the cardinal principals of any System.[8]

Joseph Pentecoste, a black pyschologist, is equally critical of this insiduous attempt to portray the black experience on television.

It would seem that the day of naked
brutality in Black-white relations
is in its nadir and anew, infinitely
more subtle and scientific strategy is
in its experimental stage. The day of
forcible rape is ending, the day of sta-
tutory rape is here. The consent is being solicited in our own living rooms.[9]

And while the movies once depicted blacks as minstrel types or being subservient foils to mythical white heroes, like Tarzan, now black cinema characters are seen as extraordinary humans who somehow always overcome their adversity through miraculous deeds.

In recent years there has been an upsurge in movies that allege to mirror some aspect of the Black Experience. The movie industry belatedly discovered that blacks made up a sizeable number of its consumership and, undoubtedly, had no reservations in exploiting this market. As a result, black movies have become tremendous box office attractions and movies like "Shaft", "Sweet Sweetback" and "Superfly" have all grossed over fifteen million dollars each. While some people, including many blacks, may see this vogue as being a progressive step toward amalgamating blacks into the predominant-ly lily-white movie industry. I feel that black people should seriously weigh the broader ramifications of what this commercial trend means in terms of identifying certain images. First, are these new movies actually representative of the Black Experience or do they simply mimick white people's interpretation of our lives? Second, do these films serve a meaningful purpose to black people or help to give us a clearer analysis of ourselves as a disenfranchised people? Third, are these films merely being produced as tonic to pacify black people and exploit the enthusiasm we have to see ourselves on screen? Fourth, do the images now being presented in black movies provide us with something more positive than what we have been exposed to in the past?

Few of the new black movies feature family themes or deal with common day to day experiences which make up the lives of most black people. Instead, they either border on the spectacular or the ridiculous. Apparently, the movie industry feels that these extremes are necessary to market black films. Consequently, black films are adulterated with an excessive amount of sex and violence to assure that they will attract large audiences.

But the most disheartening thing about the new black movies is the negative image which they portray. These movies not only re-enforce earlier stereotypes of black people (savage black, contented slave, noble slave, etc.) but they have created a set of new ones which are equally as slanderous. Some of these new images are:

Super Nigger -	("Shaft," "Sweetback," "Nigger Charley," "Hammer" and "Slaughter")
Stupid Militant -	(As seen in "Cotton Comes To Harlem" and "Bus Is Coming")
Celebrated Hustler -	("Superfly", "Cool Breeze", "Sweetback" and "Come Back Charleston Blue")
Sexual Animal -	("Sweetback", "Superfly" and "Slaughter")

In real life, there are blacks who may incorporate some of the above-mentioned characteristics. But in black movies these characteristics become wholes instead of fragments; thereby narrowing their range to one dimensional subjects.

Although it is too early to judge the full impact black movies have on black youth, one survey made of three hundred and ninety black high school students in North Lawndale can provide us with some clues. Following are the responses from two of the ten questions polled in the survey.[10]

WHICH TWO MOVIES DID YOU ENJOY THE MOST?

MOVIE	FARRAGUT		PROVIDENCE-ST. MEL		TOTAL
	M	F	M	F	
Sweet Sweetback	10	10	6	2	28
Cool Breeze	1	1	2	3	7
Slaughter	26	15	8	14	63
Blacula	9	5	6	17	37
Shaft's Big Score	7	9	3	7	26
Shaft	20	21	15	20	76
Legend of Nigger Charley	11	13	3	7	34
Superfly	46	46	49	30	171
Georgia, Georgia	0	—	0	—	—
Melinda	14	8	15	10	47
Man and Boy	1	—	1	—	2
Cotton Comes to Harlem	11	10	12	6	39
Buck & The Preacher	2	12	6	1	21
Sounder	1	1	0	—	2
Is The Father Black Enough?	6	—	1	—	7
Charleston Blue	10	9	19	6	44
Hammer	3	1	3	1	8
Lady Sings the Blues	16	27	7	10	60
The Final Comedown	2	2	9	5	18

LIST OTHER(S) NOT SHOWN:*

Trouble Man	8	7	1	0	16

* *Only movies which received 10 or more responses were listed.*

WHICH TWO MOVIES WERE POSITIVE TO YOU?

MOVIE	FARRAGUT		PROVIDENCE-ST. MEL		TOTAL
	M	F	M	F	
Sweet Sweetback	4	7	2	1	14
Cool Breeze	5	2	2	1	10
Slaughter	13	9	9	8	39
Blacula	5	4	5	8	22
Shaft's Big Score	5	3	0	2	10
Shaft	9	12	10	16	47
Legend of Nigger Charley	9	9	6	—	24
Superfly	18	30	18	19	85
Georgia, Georgia	1	0	0	2	3
Melinda	6	2	6	8	22
Man and Boy	—	2	1	—	3
Cotton Comes to Harlem	8	6	11	9	34
Buck & The Preacher	3	13	6	4	26
Sounder	1	2	1	0	4
Is The Father Black Enough?	2	2	1	—	5
Charleston Blue	3	7	5	2	17
Hammer	1	1	2	1	5
Lady Sings the Blues	10	18	5	11	42
The Final Comedown	6	2	4	—	12

LIST OTHER(S) NOT SHOWN:*

Trouble Man	2	3	0	1	6
Farewell Uncle Tom	1	2	1	1	5
Learning Tree	2	4	1	0	7

*Only those movies which received at least 5 responses were listed.

The results from this survey clearly show that respondents were quite receptive to black movies and enjoyed the ones which featured the greatest amount of violence, sex and savory lifestyles. These results can also be confirmed by the recent trends in clothing fashions which are taken from some black movies. In particular, the Superfly image has become a favorite among many black youths who seem to get gratification from straightening their hair, wearing big hats, long coats and shoes with high heels. But it is not the clothes which is the most distressing thing but the negative lifestyles associated with them.

NEGRO BOURGEOIS REVISITED

Middle class blacks, who could serve as positive models, fail to assume these roles. Those who work in the black ghetcolony flee its boundaries after five p.m., and the few who live there move when the first opportunity arises. Many of these people, politicians, businessmen, teachers and social workers, only become administrators who function contrary to the best interest of black youth. In fact, it is not uncommon for these administrators of neo-colonialism to view the black ghetcolony with as much disgust as do their white oppressors. Nathan Hare in *Black Anglo Saxons* and E. Franklin Frazier in *Black Bourgeois* have both made strong indictments on the ineptness and disconcern of the black middle class to recognize its responsibility to the larger and more oppressed black lower class. The self-imposed alienation of the black middle class from the black lower class has, unfortunately, developed a schism between them which finds the former group often indentifying with and supporting the white racist values which oppress the latter group. Many black professionals seek employment outside the black ghetcolony because jobs in the "downtown area" are more lucrative and many don't care to be associated with "those niggers anyway." Also many skilled blacks are diverted from working in the ghetcolony by large corporations which are seeking "token niggers" to showcase their professed liberalism.

The black middle class do possess many resources, both financial and skill oriented, which could help improve the quality of life for black youth. Yet in North Lawndale few members from this group ever share their resources with the community, although most of their positions have come about as a result of the social disorders that erupted in the streets. And to augment their salaries some become "white collar pimps" who serve as pacification consultants to big businesses and government agencies. The maintenance of oppression is a very lucrative business and the black professional has become the middle manager for assuring that it remains a profitable enterprise.

RUN NIGGER RUN: BUT DON'T TALK

Although many black professional athletes have captured the imagination of ghetcolony youths, these illustrious figures are usually only seen on television or at annual ghetcolony sport banquets where they regurgitate magnanimous speeches about character building and how great it is to be an American. Black professional athletes, if they ever began to recognize their accountability to the black community, could provide black youths with strong leadership. But these national heroes seem more concerned with maintaining their national image than with the problems in the black ghetcolony. Despite white society's exploitation of their talents, they fail to see themselves in any roles other than as gladiators. Legendary black heroes, like Jack Johnson, Josh Gibson, Satchel Paige, Jesse Owens and the impeccable Brown Bomber, Joe Louis, have all been subjected to the indignities of racist promoters who only recognized them as employed slaves who were able to fill their stadiums with spectators. Yet the outstanding feats of these men never gained them the monetary or social status awarded to their white counterparts (Babe Ruth, Jack Dempsey, Gene Turney, etc.). There have been a few, Jackie Robinson, John Carlos, Alex Johnson, Harry Edwards, Abdul Kareem Jabbar and the courageous Muhammed Ali, who have publicly spoken out against the tyranny of white America, but their voices are dwarfed by the hundreds who remain silent.

Recently we have seen some evidence where the black athelete is beginning to become more vocal in political affairs. This was vividly characterized by the black athletes who united with other African nations to boycott the participation of Zimbabwe (Rhodesia) in the politically maligned 1972 Olympics. The actions of these athletes were commendable, and showed the world that blacks can do more than hit home runs, make touchdowns, score forty points a game and run like gazelles with amazing ease.

There is a need for a radical re-ordering of models in the black ghetcolony. The black ghetcolony needs positive models that can be felt on the streets and throughout its total environment. It needs strong models which can show black children how to stand proud and firm and face their oppression head on, instead of turning their frustration inwardly and against their fellow blacks. It needs models which can exemplify a new system of values that denounces the "plantation mentality" of the black ghetcolony and advocates the building of a more humane community through concerted power and self-determination.

Why has it been so difficult for the black ghetcolony to develop these models? Simply because the system of oppression is structured to perpetuate self-defeating and self-destructive models. Through its racist institutions, white America is able to maintain control over black people and dictate what values and lifestyles it will accept, tolerate, suppress or destroy.

What are these institutions and how have they been able to keep black people in a form of slavery, even after the Emancipation

Proclamation allegedly set them free? The following chapters will begin to explore the modus operandi of institutional racism. We should see how this social system of authorized oppression affects the black child during his formative years.

SUBJECTS TAUGHT BY INSTRUCTORS
OF THE STREET INSTITUTION

THE MILITANT

physical education
politics
social science
armaments
administration
group dynamics

THE HUSTLER

mathematics
perception
ingenuity
creativity
exploitation
selfishness
economics
social science
verbal manipulation

THE STREET MAN

physical education
sex/biology
self defense
skill with hand weapons
aggressiveness
independence
verbal manipulation

THE PIMP

fashions
mathematics
exploitation
economics
sex/biology
verbal manipulation

THE GANG LEADER

group dynamics
physical education
team work
organization
skill with weapons
politics
loyalties
aggressiveness
obedience
conformity
fighting ability
sex/biology

THE WORKING MAN

perserverance
patience
obedience
conservatism
indifference
respect
loyalties

CHAPTER SIX

THE MIS-EDUCATION OF BLACK CHILDREN

> The United States of America permitted the enslavement of millions of black folk and then freed them in ignorance and poverty. From that day to this there has been no systematic attempt to give the masses of those people systematic elementary training. It is time to make such an attempt.
>
> W. E. B. DuBois

itutional racism. it
st indoctrinated to
a veil for America's
n these institutions
e concept of himself
schools which place
sooner does he enter
ith the symbols of
prepare him to be an
His orientation begins
giance and then, to the
g Francis Scott Key's
ly there are glamorous
efferson and Abraham
portraits of .... ce in his school, as a
Lincoln hanging in some com......
reminder of the achievements these men rendered to mankind. And
each morning the American flag is proudly raised in front of his
school to signify the land of the free and home of the brave, while in
his community no one is really free and bravery is not praised but
lived. And the remainder of his early years are saturated with the
noble legends of the founding fathers, Daniel Boone and Davy
Crockett, the romanticism of America's free enterprise system, the
justification for black slavery, learning Mother Goose rhymes and
reading an array of white fantasies, ranging from "Snow White and
the Seven Dwarfs" to the charming escapades of "Goldilocks",
"Little Red Riding Hood" and "Cinderella". And when time
permits he is taught the three R's of education, but they are
secondary to his orientation of white history and white mythology.

The public school system in Chicago is among the country's
worst, which means that the schools in its black ghetcolonies are
among the most atrocious. This fact has been documented by so
many studies that it is almost senseless to challenge its authenticity.
And though volumes of studies have been written about black
ghetcolony schools, little has been been done to improve them.
School administrators, politicians and businessmen are still
dragging their heels while black children are further being subjected
to an inferior education.

School District Ten in Chicago, which serves most of North
Lawndale, is deteriorating so rapidly that the majority of its schools
are already bordering on the brink of destruction and humiliation.
Its high schools are like incendiary factories and its elementary
schools resemble caricatures of Disneyland. Some of the incidents
which occur in North Lawndale schools defy description.

A white fourth grade teacher in one school partially burned the penis of a black child, because the student refused to comply with his homosexual advances.

In another school, a white fifth grade teacher pushed a ten year old girl down two flights of stairs because the girl failed to turn in her homework.

At one of the upper grade centers, a student was pistol whipped by a black policeman, because the student was caught smoking a reefer in the bathroom.

And in sixth grade room, a white teacher made a student sit in a seat covered with glue, because the youth was, allegedly, disturbing other class members.

A teacher in an EMH (Educable Mentally Handicapped) class allowed his students to take amphetamines, because he feels it relaxes their nerves.

A senior student was shot in the abdomen while walking through the corridors of a high school, the victim of a gang member's bullet.

A white counselor pink slipped a seven-year-old boy to a retarded school because the youth is a disciplinary case, and he can think of no other way to deal with the problem.

And each day the minds of thousands of other black students are being constantly damaged by the malicious insults of teachers and an antiquated school system which ignores their right to have a quality education.

Schools in North Lawndale are not structured to enhance a student's life, but to stifle it in such a way that only a few will ever recover from their traumatic impact. And it is tragic enough that black children in North Lawndale have to endure deteriorating school buildings, irrelevant curriculums, extreme punitive measures and political exploitation but their calamity is heightened by the caustic and ambivalent attitudes of many school teachers. Too often we tend to overlook the teacher's accountability in the academic fiasco which maligns the public schools. It is easier to blame everything on the system and, therefore, the teachers are often spared of criticism. But the classroom is still the major stimuli for the learning experience and the rapport and relationship a teacher has with students can do much to compensate for the deficiencies in the system itself. However, most administrators who teach in the ghetcolony are so mixed up themselves that it becomes almost impossible for them to do either. Instead they bring to the classroom a set of conflicting values, emotional problems and personal hang-ups which, as one would expect, do little to improve the learning potential of their students. The administrators who teach in North Lawndale can be categorized as the following types: 1) the Benevolent Misfit, 2) the Frustrated Cynic, 3) the Confirmed Racist, 4) the Social Technician, 5) th Bureaucratic Freak and 6) the Social Advocate.

THE BENEVOLENT MISFIT

The Benevolent Misfit is motivated by a puritanical compulsion to save mankind from the sorcerers of evil. He laments about all of society's evils without being able to correct any of them. He views black children as unfortunate victims who must be saved from their dark world of ignorance. In fact, the Benevolent Misfit will teach in no other area but a black ghetcolony because he feels that it is here he can best uplift the souls of the oppressed. He tries desperately to relate to his students but his orientation to white middle class values and his *victorian ideals* make it impossible for him to even begin to identify with them. He spends much of his time lamenting about how badly black children are treated and though he is in sympathy with their problems, he lacks the power and understanding to help them overcome their plight. In the classroom he is easily exploited by students because in his zest to be paternalistic he allows them unlimited freedom to do whatever they please. Although he is committed to teaching, he actually teaches very little, for he spends much of his time trying to resolve unresolvable problems. But like other missionaries who invade the black ghetcolony to help rescue the oppressed from further damnation, the Benevolent Misfit never realizes his own shortcomings. While his intentions may appear august, the Benevolent Misfit only adds to the confusion of the black child. His preachings have little influence on their behavior and his enthusiasm to appease them only accentuates their lack of discipline. Thus, the black child receives little guidance from the Benevolent Misfit except, perhaps, to be reminded that if he is to be saved from his misery it will be due to the sanctimonious generosity of the "great white father."

THE FRUSTRATED CYNIC

The Frustrated Cynic is usually a black teacher who is repulsed by being assigned to teach in a black school. He is thoroughly dissatisfied with teaching black students and would much rather teach in a school where the environment is more conducive to white middle class values. The Frustrated Cynic would really like to be employed in another profession but, because he only holds a teaching certificate, he is compelled to teach school. He is usually a harsh disciplinarian who is insensitive to the problems of his students. He feels because he has played the game according to the rules and has achieved a certain degree of success that his students need only do the same. Although he may be the product of a black ghetcolony, he no longer identifies with it and has now become a servant to white values. The Frustrated Cynic holds his students responsible for being unmotivated and unresponsive to learning and completely ignores the social conditions which influence their behavior. He is generally a chronic complainer and is contemptuous of anyone, including parents, who challenges his authority. Rarely does he stress the importance of black culture, for he has long accepted the position that black people can best achieve success by aspiring to white values.

The Frustrated Cynic does considerable harm to black children by constantly allowing his own hang-ups to influence his relationship with them. In fact, many times he sees black students as obstacles to his own progress because he feels that his professional career is being jeopardized by the backlash of the black revolt. Whereas the Frustrated Cynic could be a positive model for black children, he only re-enforces the negative concepts which so many black children develop during their formative years. His presence in black schools is even more detrimental to the educational development of black children than the Benevolent Misfit, the Racist or the Social Technician, because as a black person he only gives added credence to the larger society's racist belief that black children are basically inferior.

THE CONFIRMED RACIST

The Confirmed Racist makes no attempt to hide his dislike of black children. He openly flaunts his racism by constantly denouncing and belittling their behavior every opportunity he gets. Unlike the Frustrated Cynic, he enjoys teaching black children because it gives him the opportunity to chauvinize his white superiority. He does everything possible to make his students believe that they lack the mental capacity to become anything other than servants of white America and that their oppression stems from the incapacity of black people to compete with white people on an equal basis. He discourages black students in the pursuit of professional careers, and, instead, advocates that they aspire for short term goals as common laborers. The Confirmed Racist's treatment of black students is dehumanizing, for to him they are mere objects to ridicule and manipulate. His teaching tactics re-enforce all of the racist beliefs that have been manufactured by educational racism, and he makes every effort to demean anything that promotes black pride. His demeanor is at all times authoritarian and he is quick to exploit the low self esteem which many black students have by making them feel that whites are the major achievers in this society. He is especially harsh to those students who challenge his authority, and constantly intimidates them with racial sneers and insults.

The Confirmed Racist is always arrogant toward black parents and uses his position to make them feel ashamed when counseling them about their children. His attitude toward other teachers is equally belligerent and he constantly tries to influence school policy to exercise greater discipline over students. While the school serves as the cradle for white institutional racism, the Confirmed Racist functions as its prime nurturer to assure that its policies are implemented.

THE SOCIAL TECHNICIAN

The Social Technician uses the black school as a laboratory to test certain hypotheses and to enhance his claim as an authority on black people. His only motivation for teaching black children is to use them as guinea pigs as he explores various scientific experiments, ranging from measuring the intellectual capacities of his students to testing them for their emotional attitudes toward masturbation. To him the classroom is only a test tube to manipulate students for his own intellectual gratification. He has no interest in really teaching black students except as an exercise to experiment with different educational theories. His philosophy of teaching is centered around using technical apparatus and his classroom is always filled with the latest educational gadgets which are supposed to improve a student's learning. He maintains all types of charts and records and spends more of his time analyzing them than he does in teaching his students.

The Social Technician is usually a white liberal, though at times he may be black, who feels that by teaching black children he is making a contribution to social research. More than likely he will accumulate as much data as possible about his students for the latent intent of writing a book or professional paper on some aspect of black behavior. He is also unconventional in appearance and takes pride in being an outspoken advocate for the oppressed. The Social Technician is well read on black ghetcolony life and enjoys spending time in the black community after school. He does allow his students considerable freedom in the classroom and, under the guise of liberalism, is able to establish close relations with them. At times he invites students to his home or goes out of his way to do small things for them. However, he is not paternal in the sense that the Benevolent Misfit is, because any good will he shows toward his students is for his vested interest. The thing most damaging about the Social Technician is that in his quest for personal esteem he subordinates the things black children need for their gratification.

THE BUREAUCRATIC FREAK

The Bureaucratic Freak is addicted to regulations. He only functions as the system tells him to function and is a loyal servant to whatever it advocates. In school the Bureaucratic Freak attempts to teach black students exactly as he was taught to teach children, when he was in college. Despite the fact his college training has ill-prepared him to teach black students, he insists on using conventional teaching methods. The Bureaucratic Freak is determined to be a model teacher and does everything according to prescribed procedures. All of his teaching is done with approved textbooks and he is completely at a loss when confronted by a student who poses a question which cannot be answered by the text. His lesson plans, bulletin boards, attendance records and classroom materials are always in tact. But still his students fail to learn. The Bureaucratic Freak tries to do things so correctly and in keeping with school policy until he emerges as a completely uncreative, teaching is basically a skills oriented profession and fails to acknowledge the need for human relations techniques. He is not altogether racist like the Confirmed Racist, nor paternalistic like the Benevolent Misfit, or disgruntled like the Frustrated Cynic, or inquisitive like the Social Technician. While he tries to show respect for students, his rigidity makes him appear impersonal. In fact, the Bureaucratic Freak tries to do things so correct and in keeping with school policy until he emerges as a completely uncreative, unresourceful, unimaginative robot. The ironic thing about the Bureaucratic Freak is that he helps to perpetuate a racist school system, not out of belief but out of his obsession for conformity.

THE SOCIAL ADVOCATE

The Social Advocate can be either white or black although he is usually the latter. He is a person who has committed himself to social change. Unlike the Benevolent Misfit, whose motivation to help others is more romantic, the Social Advocate takes a practical approach to his work. He realizes that he cannot change the entire society but can effect the lives of a few children. In the classroom he tries to teach black children the things they should know about themselves and about the world around them. He exposes them to relevant materials and allows his students to participate in policy-making decisions. He talks freely about things which are wrong in society, never moralizing, and encourages his students to engage in functional projects. In discussing Civics he may invite a local politician to class, if he can coerce one into coming, and also a member from a militant organization so that students can get a broader perspective of a particular problem. He lets his students know that the school system is not working in their behalf and attempts to do something to change this situation. The Social Advocate is usually a member of an activist group and his advocacy is not confined to the schools but is evident in the community too.

Undoubtedly, black children would have a better chance to achieve under the Social Advocate. But these teachers are few and rare and it is almost inevitable that at one point in their careers they will be flushed out of the system. Institutional racism realizes that in order for its doctrine to function it cannot maintain people in its structure who happen to be advocates of truth and justice.

While these types may vary to some degree and even overlap, they do reflect attitudes of teachers which greatly contribute to the poor education of black children. It is little wonder then that black children develop a sense of alienation in the schools. Many of them feel unwanted and insecure and, therefore, respond to the classroom setting with hostility. Much of the antagonism exhibited by black students is merely a reaction to the offensive treatment they receive from teachers. And it is this kind of adverse behavior which makes many appear unmotivated and uninterested in learning and achievement.

The caustic attitudes of teachers are not the only reasons black children have so much difficulty in school. Overcrowded classrooms, poor equipment, inadequate facilities, high teacher turnover and political manipulation add to his chagrined situation.

POLITICAL FOOTBALL

In Chicago politics play a most important role in the destruction of black school children. Beginning with the Chicago School Board, whose members are appointed by Mayor Daley, to the involvement of self-interest community organizations, the skulduggery of politics is constantly being exercised at the expense of black children. In particular, the power struggle to place certain ethnic members on the school board always find black children on the losing end of the battle. Even well-intentioned community organizations will exploit black children to further their own cause. And during teachers' strikes, community boycotts and attacks on school administrators, it is the black child who usually becomes the scapegoat. The same teachers who will chastise black children in the classrooms will encourage these students to support their strike demands, which usually means helping the teachers receive bigger salaries. When community organizations wage boycotts against schools, students are told to stay home but little is done to help them make up the class time they lose while being out of school. And though there is a need to dispose of racist administrators,, I seriously question the manner in which certain community organizations manipulate the assistance of black students to confront these adversaries. For when the efforts of community self-determination fail to accomplish their goals, it is the black student who must face the reactionary treachery of these administrators. Community organizations which are truly concerned with helping black school children should be the vanguard for dealing with school crises and not subject the young to bear this responsibility. Admittedly, some of the gains made to bring about quality education for black children have been due to their courage to cross picket lines and be puppets for various bussing programs. But the vigilance needed to assure that schools are being properly managed in the interest of black children must be a responsibility of the adult community.

Fortunately, North Lawndale does have one adult organization, The Concerned Parents of Lawndale, which has attempted to make the schools accountable to the community. Under the inspirational leadership of Mrs. Ida Mae Fletcher, this group has been instrumental in bringing about greater community involvement in school affairs, the selection of principals and the revision of school curriculum. But even the efforts of this hard working group have fallen short in affecting the overwhelming deficiencies of the schools in District Ten.

THE EXILES

Because of their inability or lack of concern to cope with so-called problem students, the schools obligingly put in exile those students who do not conform to their standards. Black youth in North Lawndale drop out or are forced out of schools at an alarming rate due to a number of trivialities and misdemeanors. And the schools are assisted in this form of legal purgation by a state legislature bill which permits a teacher to suspend a youth from class up to thirty days at a time. Of course, there exists a state legislature bill that makes it mandatory for all youths to attend school until they have reached their seventeenth birthday. At the elementary school level this only means that problem students remain on the official class rolls, though they may spend the majority of their time out of school. At the high school level problem students can be suspended for an indefinite period by being sent to a continuation school which is still affiliated with the formal school system. But a student need only attend a continuation school once a week to retain formal status and for all intents and purposes he, too, becomes an exile.

And for the more serious problem students, there is the Montefiore School which is suppose to rehabilitate students so they can, hopefully, re-enter the formal school. But this school accomplishes very little in changing attitudes because it is operated on a punitive philosophy that only re-enforces a student's negative attitude toward learning. Then there is the Boys Parental Home where habitual truant boys are sent. Here boys are placed under quasi-confinement until it is felf they are more enthusiastic about attending school on a frequent basis. There are also a number of so-called vocational schools to accomondate those students who seemingly lack interest in formal school studies and who do not qualify for the other schools. At these crude replicas of outdated training centers, students are prodded along, receiving little significant education, until they graduate with no apparent skills to enter the labor market.

Once a black student is placed in exile, his chances for returning to school are extremely remote. Instead he becomes just another drop-out statistic whose fate the school system will bear no responsibility for, except to say that it did open its door to another black ghetcolony youth. Needless to say, it never admits that it also closed this same door.

THE IQ TEST: A RACIST NORM

Some educators feel that one reason many black students fail to achieve in the public schools is because of their alleged low mental capacities. This racist assumption has historically been used as a scientific explanation to explain why some black students do not fair as well on national achievement tests as most white students. Despite mountains of data which substantially refutes the theory of black inferiority, the issue continues to be one which is challenged and debated in the educational arena. Even though most educators will admit that the IQ test is skewed to represent the learning experiences of white middle class students, they, nonetheless, insist it has merit in measuring the intelligence of black students. The standards of the dominant white ruling class automatically become the norm for achievement. Although political and economic exploitation are the cornerstones of oppression, the system of oppression gains its greatest leverage over the oppressed by giving credibility to its alleged superiority. By manufacturing this image of itself, the system of oppression hopes to psyche the oppressed into believing that they are, indeed, inferior, and, therefore, deserving of their low status in the social order. After making the oppressed feel inferior, the system of oppression then pretends to be concerned with the oppressed by providing them with an education that is suppose to make them equal. But the education which the oppressed receives never gains them equality; instead it only reaffirms the oppressor's status as being superior.

Once a black student's IQ is logged on his record, the teacher makes little effort to determine its validity. The student either becomes a slow learner, a fast learner or is heaped into some other type of abstract classification. As a result, the teacher never sees the student as a total being but rather as a statistic based on norms which are suppose to reflect his learning capabilities. The student, in turn, is somehow able to detect this screening process and invariably finds himself conforming to its pattern. The slow learner continues to be a slow learner because he has been pre-identified as a slow learner. His motivation to overcome this stigma is likewise impeded because his school environment provides him with no incentive to challenge the assumptions which govern his learning experience.

In the 1969 winter edition of the *Harvard Educational Review,* Dr. Arthur R. Jensen, a professor of educational psychology and research at the University of California published an article that once again renewed the racist theory of black inferiority. His article entitled "How Much Can We Boost IQ and Scholastic Achievement" firmly suggested that black students were inferior due to their genetic composition, and that it was an exercise in futility to try and raise their IQ's. Ignoring such variables as environmental factors, motivational level, economic status and test readiness, Professor Jesen formed his conclusions on the low scores achieved by a bias sampling of black students in national IQ tests. And more recently, Professor William Shockley of Stanford University, a professor in physics, who in 1956 shared the Nobel Prize, has made similar claims of genetic deficiencies in black students. Dr. Schockley's racist theory not only supports Dr. Jensen's conclusions but goes so far as to suggest that the IQ's of black students can only be improved if blacks acquire genes from whites. While both of these theories could be interpreted as being only the hypothesis of two men, the status which Dr. Jensen and Dr. Shockley enjoy in the white academic world make them experts whose influences are widely felt among school administrators.

My criticism of Dr. Jensen and Dr. Shockley is no attempt to cover-up the fact that a large percentage of black students do score low on national IQ tests. And it is true that few enter high school with the necessary skills which are needed for academic achievement. I am also aware that those students who do continue through high school seldom recover from these disabilities. And even the few who attend college find themselves still lacking in basic academic skills. But does this mean that black students are intellectually inferior? Or is it just another indication that the public schools make no serious effort to educate black students? The second question appears closer to the truth because, as I have already suggested, it is not in the interest of the oppressor to properly educate the oppressed. The racist theory of black inferiority loses its professed credibility when one takes into account that black children exhibit a remarkable capacity for learning in the Street Institution. Though the courses in the Street Institution are structured differently than those taught in the public school, they still place great demands on a student. And most black youths are capable of acquiring that essential body of knowledge. One must examine these variances very closely if he is to understand the implications which underlie this ambivalence. Because black children are exposed to two learning environments, they must establish priorities to determine which one is more important for them to succeed in. Black children will generally try to achieve in the Street Institution because it plays such a dominant role in their lives and they have little enthusiasm for meeting the public school's requirements. Also, they usually feel alienated from the public school and find more gratification in making it in the streets. This interpretation is by no means intended to discredit the value of a relevant formal education, but only to suggest that educational achievement must be understood in terms of the situations which create different levels of motivation. If black children are to be properly educated we cannot allow them to be measured by standards which are extracted from the racist theories of their oppressor. Oppressed people will never achieve real freedom if their liberation is dependent upon achieving the standards of those who oppress them. Instead they will only become more like their oppressor and consequently forfeit their chances for ever overcoming oppression. Education for oppressed people must be shaped from their experiences and its norm for achievement must mitigate the racist theory of black inferiority. Once we bury the ludicrous notion that black children are inferior, then, perhaps, we can proceed to develop schools which can motivate them to learn in the same manner the Street Institution teaches them to survive.

INTEGRATED EDUCATION: A MISNOMER

When the United States Supreme Court made its decision in 1954 that "segregated schools are inherently unequal," implied in this decision was the fact that integrated schools were equal. But no where in its appeal for school desegregation did it comment on the effects racism had on black children. It has generally been assumed by those who advocate integrated education that schools which serve white and black children are void of racism. But the fact of the matter is institutional racism permeates the entire public school system and equally affects those schools that are segregated and those schools that are intergrated. The public school system in America was created out of the need to preserve white supremacy. For the European cast-offs who settled in America, it was imperative that they establish themselves as the dominant group so that their enslavement of black people and persecution of the Indians could be justified in intellectual terms. A perusal of textbooks used in public schools will reveal them to have a point of view that is dramatically skewed in favor of WASP's interpretation of the world. White America created an educational system to serve the interest of white people. And when events in history made it necessary to educate black people, white America made no effort to adapt its system of education to meet the unique needs of black people. Black people had little choice but to accept this racist system, and become brainwashed to a body of western thought that held itself superior over all others.

It is senseless to debate the merits of an integrated education as opposed to a segregated education when both are products of the same racist educational system. And even so-called quality education does not change the basic racist philosophy which governs the public school system. While quality education may improve the achievement scores of black students, it will not provide them with a frame of reference which reflects their culture and history. Improving a child's ability to read a racist text is by no means advancing that child's understanding of himself.

It is my contention that black children should not have to shuttled around to different communities to prove they have h minds. There is no reason why black ghetcolony children sh be able to learn as well in their community. Relocating black children to white middle class communities is just another way of telling them that their own community is inferior. In fact, to my thinking, the whole concept of integrated education is racist, for it, too, expouses the rationale that black children can only achieve when they are in the presence of whites. Exponents of integrated education always seem to feel that the growth of black children will be stymied unless they are allowed to interact with white children and be exposed to white values. Yet other ethnic groups such as Jews, Chinese and Greeks have maintained ethnic schools without sacrificing their children. Integrated education does not nullify racism, but, instead, only allows it to operate more promiscuously under the 1960's civil rights banner of black and white deceptiveness. Dista G. Caldwell, who was once a director of teacher training at Bethune Cookman College, also detects a discrepancy in this concept.

> It is a fallacy to think that forcing mixed schools in any section by the aid of the law will break down the spirit in the white American people which makes segregation in any realm of life possible. If Negro children are put into mixed schools against the will of the majority group, that same spirit which made the whites resent the presence of Negro children will lead to discrimination in the use of equipment, within the mixed school. In many elementary and high schools, Negro children are discouraged from taking courses and participating in group activities which demand group proximity of person. No form of discrimination is so deadening as that spirit substance which one cannot quite put his finger on, but which one feels in the atmosphere. The minority member gets it in a quick glance of the eye, or on the other hand, feels it in over-solicitation and patronage. Hence, forcing mixed schools in no way removes the evil effects of discrimination.[1]

The Black Muslims in America have proved that black children can learn in a totally black environment. Their schools, which serve members of the Islamic faith, operate on a year round basis, have none of the problems that plague the public schools. And more important, their students are meeting national standards and developing educational attitudes which place emphasis on the black man's culture and achievements instead of pandering to the western world's educational values.

The Honorable Elijah Muhammed, Messenger of the Black Muslims, outlines the purpose of the Muslim school:

> My people should get an education which will benefit their own people and not an education adding to the "storehouse" of their teacher. We need education, but an education which removes us from the shackles of slavery and servitude. Get an education, but not an education which leaves us in an inferior position and without a future. Get an education, but not an education that leaves us looking to the slavemaster for a job.[2]

Under a system of institutional racism it does not matter what kind of schools you have; whether they are separate schools, integrated schools, magnet schools, community controlled schools, centralized schools, decentralized schools, park schools, camp schools or schools which choose not to be called schools, black children will still be victimized.

THE AMERICAN FAILURE: A DELIBERATE PARADOX

America has yet to atone for her failure to provide an adequate education for the majority of black people. While it is able to spend billions of dollars annually to perpetuate chaos throughout the world and design modern technology that make Buck Rogers and Flash Gordon appear like amateur spacemen, it continues to allow millions of black children to endure an educational system that is decaying from the roots. Carter Godwin Woodson, the outspoken black scholar and historian, was aware of this travesty when he noted:

> In the first place, we must bear in mind that the Negro has never been educated. He has merely been informed about other things which he has not been permitted to do. The Negroes have been shoved out of the regular schools through the rear door into the obscurity of the backyard and told to imitate others whom they see from afar, or they have been permitted in some places to come into the public to see how others educate themselves.[3]

When one carefully examines Mr. Woodson's remarks, he cannot help but feel that the controllers of America's educational priorities are not at all sympathetic to the educational needs of black children. Perhaps, this is what one should expect in view of the racism which underlies the education morass black children have been subjected to. For decades black people have had to be dependent upon an educational system which has not only helped to destroy the minds of black children but also has helped to condition them to aspire for things the "great society" denies them in reality. Despite what black people are led to believe, education does not assure them equality in this society. Although it does allow some to have a degree of economic security, it in no way prepares them to overcome their oppression. True education for black children must be structured around liberating concepts which not only enable them to survive their community but be revolutionary and creative enough to help them change it.

Paulo Freire calls this type of education libertarian as opposed to the oppressor's system of education which he identifies as the banking concept, where the oppressed merely become repositories for the oppressor's dogma. Of course, it has never been in the interest of America to abandon its banking concept of education. Under this type of demoralizing educational system, it is highly doubtful if black children will ever receive an education that will prepare them for liberation.

> Those truly committed to liberation must reject the banking concept in its entirety, adopting instead a concept of men as conscious beings, and consciousness as consciousness intent upon the world. They must abandon the educational goal of deposit-making and replace it with the posing of the problems of men in their relations with the world.[4]

America's system of education has not really failed black people. Paradoxically, it has done exactly what is was designed to do; harness the minds of black people to a body of distorted knowledge. Black people have been led to believe that America was seriously interested in providing all of her citizens with a quality education. Having belief in the American educational system, even with all its ills, does make the oppressed feel that their oppressor is interested in their welfare. The system doesn't work for black people, but yet they feel its intentions are sincere. But the oppressor knows that his true motive for providing an education for black people is to create the very ominous situation which exists in the public school system. In fact, the oppressor will sometimes join the ranks of those who denounce his school system to show that he has compassion for their concerns. However, the system of oppression will never make any changes in its school system which will benefit black people. It is, indeed, a disparaging outlook which demands that black educators begin to seriously seek meaningful educational alternatives as a means to achieve an equitable education for black children.

A SPECT OF HOPE

There are a few schools in North Lawndale which are making an effort to save some black children from the disease of educational malnutrition. On Pulaski Road near 14th Street there is a Child-Parent Center, named after Milton Olive,Jr., a black youth who was killed in Viet Nam while saving the lives of four other soldiers, which emphasizes parent involvement and uses culturally oriented materials that are designed for black children. The school serves approximately one hundred and ninety students in the pre-kindergarten through primary grades. The Olive Child-Parent Center has achieved considerable success in teaching children how to read and its overall program appears to be far in advance of other schools in the community. A similar type school, Herzl Schome, has also been able to improve the performances of its students, comparable to national standards. An example of a pre-school that is attempting to properly educate black children is the Learning Tree, the largest private nursery school in the Midwest. At this center, which has a daily attendance of nearly three hundred, black children are exposed to a range of creative activities that will better prepare them to succeed when they enter the public schools.

There is also a special program in North Lawndale called Talented Tenth, which is co-sponsored by the Board of Education and Northeastern State University, that attempts to raise the educational level of potentially gifted students. Children are selected from various schools in North Lawndale and attend classes taught by specialists at the university's west side campus. But this experimental program does not come close to touching the thousands of other black children whose true potentials will never develop as long as their minds continue to be filled with educational debris.

And at one youth agency, the Better Boys Foundation, there is a program for students who have dropped out (or have been kicked out) of school which offers them another chance to complete their education. Unlike most schools of this kind, that are detached from the school system, this program serves as an outpost for students who are still a part of the formal school. The rationale for this type of school appears sound, for it does acknowledge the fact that certain students can best achieve in a less formal atmosphere which allows them some freedom to express themselves within the cultural norms of their own social milieu. Although the curriculum at this school does not greatly deviate from the formal school, it is staffed with teachers (Social Advocates) who are genuinely concerned with giving black youths quality education. But even the "second chance" school fails to reach the hard-core drop-out who already feels that his chances have been blown. And in most cases, he will be correct.

At this same agency, there is also a leadership training program for pre-adolescents called Project LEAD (Leadership, Educational and Development) that uses trained counselors, junior leaders and community people to strengthen a youth's development. The staff works closely with the families of each boy and helps him in those educational areas where he is most vulnerable.

The examples that I have mentioned do reflect a few programs which are attempting to improve the quality of education for black children. But the problem of mis-education in North Lawndale is so pervasive that these programs become obliterated when weighted against the glaring inefficiencies which are inherent in the Chicago public school system.

The children in North Lawndale like the children of other black ghetcolonies throughout America are the future hope of black people. The black community can ill afford to have new generations of black children become crippled adults. It is in need of too many doctors, technicians, chemists, skilled tradesmen and scientists to allow more black children to be destroyed by the educational maze of racism which infiltrates the lives of black children at kindergarten and follows them until they have been totally brainwashed into accepting oppression as though it is as American as apple pie.

CHAPTER SEVEN

THE BENEVOLENT OPPRESSOR:
MYTH OF SOCIAL SERVICE AGENCIES

> One must say that social work and
> philanthropy as instruments of
> constructive social change have so
> far had little impact in any of
> the nation's urban ghettos.
>
> *Dark Ghetto*
> Kenneth B. Clark

North Lawndale is flooded with social service agencies.

The system of oppression nurtures its paternalistic ego at the expense of the oppressed. And like all exploitive systems it rarely alters the life-chances of its victims but only sustains their oppression by making them more dependent on the system which preys upon them. Proportionately black people in Chicago make up the largest constituency of social service agencies. And by being placed in this notorious position they are categorically labeled as expendables. ADC mothers are accused of being prostitutes, the elderly treated as though their life span has already expired, the crippled looked upon as freaks, the underfed and ill clothed as parasites, the mentally retarded as deviants, the uneducated as imbeciles, the unemployed as criminals and children born out of wedlock as illegitimates. This type of dehumanization is the penalty many people pay for being poor and black.

The emergence of social service agencies in America developed from Judea-Christian ethics, the Elizabethan poor laws and the benevolent need to correct the ills of impoverished people. These agencies encompassed a philanthropic philosophy that was based upon the dignity of the individual and the premise that every man should be his "brother's keeper". But this philosophy failed to recognize the great disparity between whites and blacks and the ever-present power of the establishment to keep black people oppressed. As America grew into a technological society simultaneously there came about an increase in urban communities. With the growth of these communities migrated large numbers of people who brought with them problems that cities were unprepared to cope with. This crisis of urbanization necessitated the need for massive social service programs, both private and public, to deal with problems acutely associated with urban living. Settlement Houses, youth agencies and other welfare institutions began to provide services which attempted to minimize urban frustration and offer direct help to those people who were victimized by deprivation, unemployment and poor housing. Perhaps, for the Irish, Polish, German and other ethnic immigrants who came to the cities during this period, these services appeared realistic. For the needs of those people were basically the acquisition of social services which could help them escape a life of poverty. However, the history of the black man in America was remarkably different. Unlike the white immigrant, the black man was not trying merely to get into the mainstream of American life, but, more eventful, he was struggling to gain acceptance as a free human being. Social service agencies did not address themselves to liberation but, instead, assumed that black people's problems could be solved with the same services provided to impoverished whites. This lack of distinction made the entire social service movement a farce to black people because it could do nothing to alleviate the scars of slavery and the effects of an oppressive system that dehumanized people because of the color of their skin. The principles of social service agencies could not be fully applicable to black people because the problems of black people resulted from a political and economic system that condoned and fostered institutional racism. Nevertheless social service agencies proceeded to design programs for black people that were irrelevant to their foremost need...that of gaining freedom. Instead of looking at the black ghetcolony as a unique phenomenon, they only viewed the black man's problem as just another manifestation of poverty. Social service agencies approached all problems from a Puritan reference that was more acclimated toward pacifying human suffering than alleviating the causes which made human suffering exist.

The people who generally administrate social service programs are the social workers, youth workers, guidance counselors, caseworkers, etc. These are the social practitioners who are hired to be servants of the people, but who, instead, attempt to function as their masters. Primarily, the role of a social practitioner is that of a buffer agent whose function is to pacify the oppressed to adjust more easily to oppression. As a product of the oppressor's educational system, the social practitioner is indoctrinated with so many pathological theories about the oppressed that it becomes difficult, if not impossible, for him to practice his profession without applying these theories to his constituents. Although he may have a sincere desire to help people, his approach to their problems is based on the premise that the oppressed can be saved by merely providing them with paternalistic services. He fails to recognize that oppression is caused by political and economic interests which can never be corrected by the paternalistic services he has been trained to provide. His ignorance of this cause and effect relationship only makes him look for solutions to problems that are alleged to be caused by behavioral deficiencies and, therefore, he is unable to analyze their genesis from a political perspective. As a result, the victims of oppression who he is trying to help become the scapegoats for their own oppression. In North Lawndale there are countless numbers of these social practitioners who come to the black ghetcolony as if they were sent by God to save an uncivilized people and as one might suspect, this army of misguided paternalists attracts a large number of Benevolent Misfits, Bureaucratic Freaks and Social Technicians.

THE PRIVATE SOCIAL AGENCY: ARTIFICIAL PANACEA

The social practitioner exercises his greatest influence, or lack of influence, on the black child in the privately endowed leisure time social agencies, i.e., boys clubs, youth centers, YMCA's and settlement houses. It is in these institutions where the socialization process of the black child is supposed to be enhanced and re-enforced. All private social agencies claim to be "character builders", and "molders of responsible citizens". But to the black ghetcolony child, becoming"responsible" and developing "character only means that he must become subservient to white society's skewed code of ethics. These euphemisms are expeditious to social agencies because they do encourage donors to contribute large sums of money to their budgets. Of course, these illustrious statements are never examined for their validity, because most people contribute to charitable organizations for vested interests and not out of a genuine humanitarian concern for others.

Private social agencies are big business.

As not-for-profit institutions, they have amassed considerable wealth, property, buildings and other financial assets. Some, like the YMCA and the Boys Clubs, are chartered members of national organizations whose boards are comprised of high ranking politicians and wealthy businessmen. A perusal of the people who serve on boards of private social agencies in Chicago would read like a social register or an election ballot. But while these people are essential to the financial support of private social agencies, an examination of their other interests often reveals gross inconsistencies. Many of these board members belong to Chicago's "power elite" whose own political and economic interests often contribute to the conditions which their agencies are trying to change. While this examination may not find all members who serve on these boards to be hypocrites nonetheless, it does raise the question about who is actually helping whom.

The private social agencies which are in the black ghetcolony are almost totally dependent upon white financial support. This type of dependency does have its drawbacks when these agencies implement programs which may conflict with the interests of their benefactors. The larger black community of Chicago has yet to develop a funding source of its own similar to the Catholic Charities, Lutheran Charities and Jewish Charities. There is the Joint Negro Appeal but this small agency has not been successful in developing the administrative apparatus needed to raise large sums of money. Consequently, private social agencies in the black ghetcolony find themselves soliciting funds from some of the same sources that are responsible for the oppression of black people. The system of oppression is designed to make the oppressed dependent upon the resources of the oppressor so that the exploitation of the oppressed is buffered with paternalism.

Because it is a ghetcolony there are many paternalistic youth programs in North Lawndale. In fact, just about every new and old youth program that has been manufactured by the great society serves an apprenticeship here. And the hue and cry to save the youth of North Lawndale blares out like the number one record on Chicago's soul stations. Everybody claims to be doing something for youth. Social agencies, in particular, are the most flagrant fabricators of this propaganda. Despite the fact that black youths in North Lawndale remain caught up in an endless web of deprivation, private social agencies continue to print impressive brochures about the wonderful things their programs are doing for youth. But in reality these much acclaimed programs do little to improve the life-chances of youths who are victims of oppression.

The greatest fault of private social agencies is that they fail to intervene in the overpowering political and economic elements in the black ghetcolony which foster oppression. For the most part, these agencies only engage in non-controversial activities and seldom take a public stand on political or economic issues which effect the lives of the people they serve. The true value of a private social agency must be measured by its involvement with the total community and by how successful it is in helping to tear down the barriers that deny people opportunities for advancement. A private social agency cannot solve problems through selective bargaining, but must interact, regardless how painful, with every strata of this social system that impedes the mobility of black people. If they are to be relevant they must stop functioning as apostolic citadels of paternalism and become instigators of change which are committed to reshaping society instead of only modifying behavior. The Street Institution will continue to be the greatest influence on black youths until social agencies can begin to provide them with meaningful alternatives which better enable black youths to survive their environment.

The ineffectiveness of private social agencies to meet the needs of black youths cannot be blamed solely on them. Many do try very hard to improve the life-chances of the youths they serve. However, as private institutions they are often faced with situations which are beyond their resources, but, nonetheless, they are expected to do more than the public agencies, whose resources are far greater. The demands which the community place on private social agencies are often unrealistic and consequently these institutions become the objects of displaced aggression and hostility. In particular, many youths who have been rebuffed by public agencies find it convenient to vent their frustration and anger on private social agencies. In North Lawndale, many private social agencies were besieged by some gang members who disrupted their programs and intimidated them for jobs.

For some asinine reason, many people feel that private social agencies can be a panacea for the problems black children are confronted with in the ghetcolony. With their structured group work programs, recreational activities, arts and crafts programs, limited counseling services and annual basketball tournaments, these agencies are expected to perform miracles. In the chapter on black street gangs it was discussed how defenseless youth agencies were in actually helping those youths who have the greatest need. One reason why many black youths spend more time in the Street Institution is the lack of appeal private social agencies have for them. At best, private social agencies only accommodate the needs and interests of marginal members of the Street Institution. Despite this fact, they persist in stating otherwise because of their need to raise funds. During the height of the gang conflict in North Lawndale, many private social agencies took advantage of this situation to promote their fund raising interests. Representatives from various private social agencies would frequently travel to the white suburbs and speak to audiences about the explosiveness of the gang situation and claim that their agencies would neutralize this problem with proper funds. Some representatives would even take articulate gang members with them to make their claim more authentic. A director of one west side agency admitted that he had put together a collection of hand weapons, zip guns, knives and brass knuckles for the sole purpose of dramatizing the gang problem. And after hearing about these exciting escapades, whites willingly responded with contributions, perhaps not so much out of believing what they had heard, but because it probably eased their consciences to feel that they were helping those "culturally deprived children" get something more out of life. It is a game that has been played for years at the sacrifice of black children.

WELFARE COUNCIL

To help increase the efficiency of social agencies, coordinate their services, screen their activities, establish their priorities and standardize their procedures there is a governing bureaucracy called the Welfare Council of Metropolitan Chicago. The Welfare Council is considered the primary authority on social welfare in Chicago. Organized in 1914, its 1967 statement of purpose outlines its present role:

> To conserve and strengthen human resources in Metropolitan Chicago and facilitate the delivery of health and welfare services to people who need them, the Council shall promote and engage in social planning to influence social change.[1]

Prior to 1968, the planning by the Welfare Council involved few representatives from the black ghetto. In 1968, this lack of representation was challenged by a black group named Catalyst which placed demands on the Welfare Council to be more accountable to the black community.

> We, the Catalyst, a black organization dedicated to the liberation and welfare of all black people from the oppressive forces of this society, do hereby demand of the Community Fund its allocated budget to the Planning and Research Department of the Welfare Council of Metropolitan Chicago. This demand is being made in view of the Welfare Council's Planning and Research Department's failure and inability to provide black communities with any significant or constructive input which can help alleviate the social, economic and political injustices that are contributing to the annihilation of black people. It has become quite apparent to us that black communities can no longer allow themselves to be exploited as an excuse to raise funds which, in turn, offers them no benefits or real participation in the decision-making policies of agencies that are insensitive to their needs.[2]

At the same time the Community Fund of Chicago, which allocates funds to the Welfare Council, also questioned the performance of the Welfare Council in regard to its involvement in the black community. As a result of this criticism, the Welfare Council eventually hired more blacks to its professional staff as well as to its board of directors. But the majority of its board members continued to represent the business sector and the policies of the Welfare Council have not changed dramatically enough to make it truly accountable to the black community. Yet, its decisions will invariably influence black children, for all policies relating to social service agencies in some way affect the lives of the young.

PUBLIC AGENCIES: POLITICAL PUPPETS

If the private social agencies which serve the black youth of North Lawndale seem bad then the public agencies are abominable. While the private agencies do make an attempt to implement programs, the public agencies just write them down on paper. Public agencies dare not serve the real needs of the community. It is almost inconceivable for them to do so. Instead public agencies are only intended to lift the hopes of people and promote the program of the ruling political body. And if private agencies function as buffers, public agencies act as controllers.

COMMISSION ON YOUTH WELFARE

For many years, the dominant public youth agency in Chicago was the Commission on Youth Welfare. Formed in 1958 by the Chicago City Council, the Commission on Youth Welfare was generally recognized as being one of Mayor Daley's pet projects because it helped to give him an image of being concerned with the welfare of Chicago's youth. However, the Commission on Youth Welfare was a nebulous institution whose statement of purpose failed to clarify its role. Some of its ambiguous functions were as follows:

1) Cooperate with the mayor, the city council, city departments, agencies and officials in carrying out a *comprehensive program of youth welfare* involving all public and voluntary agencies engaged in providing services or facilities to the youth of Chicago.

2) *Recommend* such legislative action as it may deem appropriate to effectuate the policy of the Commission. The Commission shall *render an annual report* to the Mayor and the City Council.

3) *Invite,* enlist and encourage the cooperation of all voluntary agencies, racial, religious and ethnic groups, community organizations, labor and business organizations, fraternal and benevolent societies, veterans' organizations, professional and technical organizations, and *other groups* in the city of Chicago, *in carrying on its work.*

The Commission *may aid in the formation of local* community groups in such neighborhoods as it may deem necessary or desirable.

4) *Cooperate* with state and federal agencies whenever it deems such action appropriate in *effectuating the policy of the Commission.*

5) *Conduct public hearings,* carry on research or otherwise obtain factual data, issue such publications and make such recommendations as in its judgment will effectuate the policy of the Commission.[3]

At times the Commission on Youth Welfare tried to imitate the cloak and dagger exploits of the CIA. Workers from its staff would venture out into the streets and attempt to keep a photographic memory of everything that went on, especially if the activities appeared to be anti-establishment. When these workers came back to their offices they meticulously put down their impressions on reams of paper which were then neatly placed in file cabinets. The Commission on Youth Welfare did not limit its spying to just youth, but also kept a vigilant eye on controversial adults and militant organizations. Workers were able to camouflage their clandestine activities because they claimed to only be coordinating programs and acting as resources for the community. But the only activities they coordinated were those which were already over-coordinated, and as resources they could only provide what their superiors approved, which was generally limited to free baseball tickets and soda pop for a family cook-out.

In 1968, a dissonant group of predominantly black professionals attended what came to be known as the Vinzant Conference for the purpose of demanding that the Commission on Youth Welfare become responsive to the black community. Some of the allegations proposed at that meeting substantiates what has been already implied:

> Our functioning and responsibilities have been concentrated in black communities as we presently operate, we are purveyors of discriminatory and repressive practices. In fact, we have participated in intimidating existing and emergent groups by reporting participants in meetings, etc., and in working to isolate those groups which are designed or organized to develop programs to meet their community's needs as they see them. Hardly, if ever, have we made attempts to exercise the same type of activities in white communities where discrimination and repression germinate.

The agencies and/or institutions that we have been encouraged to work with are inner-directed or singleminded in their direction, i.e., the perpetuation of oppression in black and other deprived communities.

We have been manipulating communities to support legislation which the political system has deemed necessary that may not be in the best interest of the people rather than accepting responsibility for initiating legislative action.

We have cooperated and collaborated with certain programs as they develop at the local, state and federal levels, primarily local and federal, assessed the possibilities of funding; lobbied to secure funds through federal sources and in some cases established programs like, NYC and Operation Venus, within the agency.

After making its charges public, members from this caucus began to hold a series of meetings with Mayor Daley and the director of the Youth Commission. Then, as though there had never been a problem, the caucus mysteriously dissolved and the policies of the Commission once again reigned over the black community. But this abortive coup is not unusual in Chicago politics. The political machine of Chicago has a way of neutralizing even its most outspoken adversaries. The Commission on Youth Welfare operated as an appendage of City Hall. Its top administrators were all appointed with the Mayor's approval and those who hold patronage jobs in Chicago always support the programs of their benefactors.

The Commission on Youth Welfare was dismantled in 1970 and its ties to the Chicago City Council were severed. But when it was shifted to the Department of Human Resources, it remained attached to Mayor Daley's office. Under the Department of Human Resources it was renamed the Joint Youth Development Program and relocated in the Urban Progress Centers. The programs of the JYDP and the Commission on Youth Welfare differ only in that the former does not attempt to infiltrate the programs of other agencies nor does it take an active role in monitoring youth groups. Its primary function appears to be that of a resource provider to those agencies and community groups that serve as work stations to the Department of Human Resources. By far, its biggest program is the much criticized Neighborhood Youth Corps Program. The NYC serves over 50,000 youths each year who are assigned to work stations which are supposed to provide them with meaningful work experiences. Most of the youths, whose ages range from fourteen to twenty-two, receive a modest stipend of $1.68 per hour and work thirty hours a week during the summer as opposed to ten hours a week during the school year. The criticism of the NYC is not in its hiring of youths but in the types of meaningless jobs most receive. In this respect, the NYC program is utterly ridiculous as a preparatory work program that is suppose to instill in its enrollees the virtues of the "protestant work ethic". Many of the jobs which NYC enrollees undertake are so poorly supervised and unrelated to the real job market that it is impossible for them to develop positive work attitudes. Instead, many just loaf around doing nothing or are assigned to chores like cleaning up rubbed lots and dirty streets. Through no fault of their own, these youths are being paid as though the work world places no real responsibility on workers. Of course, the JYPD cannot be held solely responsible for this superficial situation. The agencies and community groups which serve as work stations are equally guilty because of their failure to program meaningful jobs for NYC enrollees. Instead, most of these agencies and groups seem content with this charitable arrangement and usually request far more enrollees than they can properly supervise. However, the Department of Human Resources complies with this apathy and makes no real effort to correct it because providing jobs for youths, no matter how irrelevant they may be, does impove its community image as a benevolent agency. And, of course, this image tends to make the community forget the other services which it promises but never delivers.

ILLINOIS DEPARTMENT OF CORRECTIONAL SERVICES

The Illinois Department of Correctional Services, once known as the Illinois Youth Commission, is almost a carbon copy of the old Commission on Youth Welfare, except that it also has legal authority over those youth adjudicated as delinquents by the juvenile courts. Formed in 1953 by the 68th Illinois General Assembly, its purpose is to provide community services for youth and to maintain supervision of correctional institutions, although the latter service tends to receive greater importance.

The Illinois Youth Commission's community service program is based upon the philosophy of the Chicago Area Project, founded byt the late sociologist, Clifford R. Shaw, in 1934. Shaw observed that it was in the high density areas where the greatest number of juvenile crimes occurred and concluded that active community participation would help decrease juvenile delinquency in overcrowded neighborhoods. While this analysis appears sound, it rarely gets a chance to be tested in the black ghetcolony. First, as a public agency, the IYC has an authoritarian image which creates anxieties among people when it is trying to help organize communities. Second, its conceptualization of community organization is more academically oriented and predisposed to the maintenance of conventional norms. Thus, you find the situation in which a public agency is functioning under restrictions that will not allow it to support certain activities of a community, even if the people deemed them necessary for their betterment. For example, one would hardly expect the IYC to support a group of rebellious parents who were determined to stage a demonstration against the governor of Illinois.

However, it is in the area of correctional service to youths that the IYC makes its presence felt in the black community. Assigned with the responsibility of maintaining supervision of all youth correctional centers in Illinois, it is no wonder its staff of probation officers, community workers and administrators frequently come in contact with black youths. But this relationship is usually not out of some deep concern for their welfare but because it is their job to do so.

Other public agencies are equally unresponsive to the real needs of black youths. They become so diluted with bureaucracy and restricted by political priorities that the average black child in North Lawndale never feels their influence or, for that matter, know they even exist.

THE GREAT SOCIETY: EXPOSED

In 1964, the Johnson administration belatedly and naively discovered that there existed in this country large populations who were not benefitting from America's great wealth. This revelation led the administration to open its dusty file cabinets in search of quick remedies to correct this disparity. What it found were the New Deal programs of the F.D.R. era and after wiping the dust off these frayed documents and making a few alterations, it proudly came up with what the great society called its War on Poverty. Thus was born America's third new deal (the first being Reconstruction), the Poverty Program. The axiom, "if it doesn't work at first then try again," typifies the manner in which the Office of Economic Opportunity was created.

In Chicago, Mayor Daley gained custodianship over its share of the Poverty Program and incorporated it under his already powerful political machine. The Chicago version of the Poverty Program was housed in Urban Progress Centers, which came to be known as little city halls. The Urban Progress Center in North Lawndale opened in

1965 and, like the other social agencies, began to make empty promises to youths. When it was not duplicating the failures of other youth programs, it was creating programs with their own built-in failures.

Then in 1967 an extended version of the Poverty Program came into being. It was called Model Cities and devoted to "Improving the quality of urban life..." in four Chicago slum communities, one of which was North Lawndale. While the Poverty Program was to alleviate poverty, Model Cities was supposed to help bring about institutional change.

> The underlying concept of a Model
> Cities Program is institutional change.
> The programs seek primarily to expand
> the minds of those in charge of institu
> tions, agencies and organizations to ac-
> cept new ideas, new techniques, new pro-
> grams and new procedures in confronting
> the new problems that constantly arise
> to challenge them in our changing urban
> society. The aim is to have viable in-
> stitutions characterized by an ability
> to consistently renew themselves through
> permanent, substantial, innovative and
> significant changes in their view of how
> they should respond to the needs of the
> community.[5]

These words taken from Mayor Daley's introduction to the Chicago Model Cities 1967 brochure would appear to have been made by a political activist seeking overthrow of the government. However, in the following paragraph of this same statement, Mayor Daley qualifies his revolutionary zeal with one of his classic ambivalent statements.

> It is possible that some of the projects
> of the Chicago Model Cities Program might
> fail in attaining their immediate and visi-
> ble goals and still succeed in achieving
> the ultimate goal of bettering our institu-
> tions.[6]

Ralph H. Metcalfe, Jr., a Chicago resident and graduate of Columbia University, made the following comments about the Chicago Model Cities Program in a critical article published in the *Black Scholar* journal.

It is the thesis of this paper that the
Model Cities Program of the City of
Chicago is a neocolonial program, seeking as its primary objective not to better the living conditions of black people,
but rather to entice them into a position
of servitude within that urban center.[7]

After expounding upon his thesis, Mr. Metcalfe concludes his
article by saying:

It is a program for the neocolonialization
of non-white human capital. Its thin veneer of attractiveness covers a policy of
political and economic domination. It is
antithetical to the best interests of the
Latin American and Afro-American communities, and should be resisted at all cost.[8]

Of course, there is another side to the Chicago Model Cities
story. Its supporters will disclaim these allegations and boast about
what it has already done and will accomplish in the future. But then
this type of allegiance should be expected when many of these same
supporters are receiving salaries well above the poverty level in this
country, to the tune of some ten to fifteen thousand dollars and
more. An article in a major Chicago newspaper revealed the
following collaborating evidence of Model Cities' huge payroll:

During the two years that the federally
funded Model Cities programs has operated here, more than $20 million has been
spent on staff salaries while the program
has virtually ignored the critical issue
of housing.

With salary expenditures of this size, it will be a major
accomplishment for Chicago's Model Cities program to preserve the
status quo, least of all, effect institutional change.

The failure of Chicago's Poverty Program vis a vis Model Cities
and the Department of Human Resources to help improve the
life-chances of black youths who live in North Lawndale is basically
due to political interest. Although the Urban Progress Center in
North Lawndale has made efforts to involve local residents in
policy-making roles, the majority of its programs are based on
decisions made by the bureaucratic caretakers of Daley's political
machine. When Mayor Daley was able to manuever government

funds for Model Cities and the Department of Human Resources to be controlled by his office, these agencies became political instruments to perpetuate his power. As I have already noted in chapter one, machine politics play an important role in the oppression of the Black ghetcolony. And even if Model Cities and the Department of Human Resources were staffed with nothing but social advocates, their services would have little impact on the oppressed as long as these agencies were linked to the very political and economic institutions which share responsibility for the oppression in the black ghetcolony.

GRASSROOT STOP GAPS

Other programs which affect the youths of North Lawndale are promoted by various churches, civic groups and community organizations. These programs range from sponsoring athletic teams, spasmodic job finding to just providing youths with another unsupervised enviroment to satisfy recreational needs. Many of these programs do have sincere intentions but lack the funds to implement more meaningful activities for youth. Others are organized around secular interests and the self-aspiring ambitions of egotists.

One youth employment program in North Lawndale is sponsored by the North Star Missionary whose director is also the "Negro spokesman" for the John Birch Society. Anyone with the slightest knowledge of this ultra conservative organization should know that it only strives to maintain the status quo. The youth in North Lawndale have already been vertically confined and will only overcome economic discrimination through an asserted horizontal attack on unemployment which can re-apportion the present racist arrangement of the job market.

Even the religious institutions fail miserably in helping black children to confront the realities in their environment. They continue to employ the age old dogmatism of advocating the purification of one's soul when there is a conspicuous absence of purity in one's community. The black Christian church tends to ignore the overt oppression that manifests itself in North Lawndale and simply conditions black children to accept their present state of life for a future experience in heaven.

Although the early black Christian church did play an important role in combating oppression, today it has replaced that resistence with compromise. Despite the fact that the black Christian church remains one of the most influential institutions in the black community, there exists little evidence of its using this influence to reject those western values which are being used to further the cause of institutional racism. The very fact that it remains a bridesmaid to Christianity relegates its role to picketing, boycotting and other types of peaceful demonstrations. Simply, today's black Christian church uses the oppressor's religion to challenge his lack of morality to uphold the doctrines which Christianity is founded upon. Obviously, this is a futile endeavor because Christianity, as practiced by most whites, has yet to be successful in changing the racist attitudes of its own converts.

The role Christianity has played in the support of slavery, discrimination and segregation cannot be casually dismissed. Christianity has failed to use its resources to correct the wrongs done to black people. On the contrary, it has conveniently used its cross and its bible as ploys to pacify black people's discontent and to neutralize their aggressiveness.

North Lawndale is saturated with black Christian churches, both conventional and storefront types, which are able to fill their pews each Sunday but are unable to provide their congregations with any constructive programs geared to help their liberation.

It is extremely unlikely that social services agencies, as they are presently structured, will ever meet the real needs of black people in America. Because this country's distribution of wealth is controlled by capitalism, which is infested with racism, it is not in its interest to deliver equitable services to black people. Captialism is one reason why there is such a wide economic gap between whites and blacks and its continued success feeds upon this disparity. Social service agencies are but a buffer to this system. They merely serve as band-aids to patch up economic sores caused by capitalism. As long as we live under a system of capitalism there will always be the haves and the have nots. And when this system conspires with racism and colonialism, black people will always be the ones who are the most exploited and oppressed. In the next chapter, I will identify those whose functions are to regulate the behavior of the oppressed so that the system of oppression can operate with little resistance.

CHAPTER EIGHT

LAW AND ORDER:
TWO STANDARDS, BLACK AND WHITE

Black people cannot be protected
by American law, for we have no
franchise in this country. If
anything, we suffer double indemni-
ty: we have no law of our own and
no protection from the law of white
America which by its intention and
by the very nature of the cultural
values which determined it is
inimical to blackness.

Black Scholar
Robert Chrisman

The summer of 1967 in North Lawndale was much like the summers in other black ghetcolonies throughout America. It, too, was in a state of insurrection. There were the familiar flames from burning buildings which only intensified the stifling ghetcolony heat; the pilfering of televisions, radios and clothes from ramshackled businesses; the hysteria of older people seeking shelter and the trigger happy reactions of over zealous policemen. And there were the bewildered black children who stood in the streets, not knowing that they were also participants in this social crisis.

A white policeman wearing a blue crash helmet stood unnerved over a prostrate boy, making defiant gestures at the throng of angry people who had congregated around him. His index finger still gripped the trigger of the shotgun that had only a few minutes earlier unloaded the devastating pellets which had penetrated the ten year old youth in his neck and thigh, sending him sprawling on the cracked pavement. According to witnesses, the boy had been playing with friends when an older youth dashed past them. A determined policemen in hot pursuit leveled his shotgun at the fleeing figure. The blast from a shotgun makes no distinction when fired randomly into a crowd of people. However, this time it did find its mark as the older youth tumbled to the ground. But the spray of pellets also hit the younger boy. The policeman had indiscreetly fired at the older youth because, allegedly, he had been seen pilfering beer from a liquor store. And, as is customary, such an act constituted a felony in the eyes of the law which knew of no other way to deal with rampaging youth who were caught up in the rage of insurrection.

Many black children met a similar fate that year in Detroit, New York, Cleveland and Newark after the 1965 holocaust of Watts had already established a precedent for policemen to be jury, judge and executioner in quelling these types of social upheavals. The police did not differentiate between a youth taking an item from a store and a sniper crouched in the corner of some dark room waiting for the right time to strike. To them, anyone who appeared to be involved in the melee of disorders that kept many cities in flames for days was a menace, even if he was only a child whose curiosity may have led him to seek excitement, as children do when they attempt to follow fire trucks or run after an ambulance that is zigzagging through the streets. But during crises like these, just being black is reason enough to be killed. A look at a few other tragic encounters between black youths and police will make this more evident.

In 1969, two black brothers, Michael and John Soto were killed in separate shootings under what are still considered to be extenuating circumstances. Michael, the youngest brother, was killed when a policeman, supposedly by accident, discharged his revolver, after stopping Michael for questioning late one night. The oldest brother, John, a sergeant in the army, was slain by another policeman while he was fleeing from an alleged hold-up. The ironic thing about John's death was that it occurred one week later, while he was on emergency leave to attend his brother's funeral.

The same year on a hot summer night, three youths were driving a stolen vehicle when a squadron with two policemen spotted them running a stop sign. A chase followed which ended with the car driven by the youths striking a lamp post. The policemen then claimed they walked over to the wrecked car to make an arrest when one youth, Johnny Johnson, age sixteen, resisted and a struggle ensued. During the encounter one officer discharged his revolver and Johnny was dead. And at the coroner's inquest for each of these shootings the verdict was justifiable homicide. But coroner's inquests are only staged to give black people a false impression that justice is being properly administered in their behalf. Yet, I maintain that most verdicts at these mocked tribunals are made long before the jury presides. Indeed, they are made when black children are born.

Finally, some youths began to react to these incidents of justifiable homicide.

In 1970, on a dark street in North Lawndale, another police squadron was cruising around, apparently making its nightly surveillance, when it was met with a barrage of gun shots. Miraculously no one was killed. A week later four youths, ranging from ten to thirteen years of age, were arrested and accused of attempted murder.

And in other areas of the city black youths were being blamed for more police shootings; one incident in the Cabrini Green Housing Project left two policemen killed, while on the South Side a task force officer was slain while seated in an unmarked car.

These are only a few of the many incidents which dramatize the schism that exists between the Chicago police and black youths. Seldom does a week go by in the black ghetcolony where a youth does not become the victim of a policeman's bullet. And many become victims simply because they were bystanders or perhaps made the unpardonable sin of committing a misdemeanor. To some policemen, shooting at black youths, regardless of the circumstances, is considered to be a part of their job description.

LAW AND ORDER: A RACIST METAPHOR

The Chicago Police Department takes considerable pride in displaying on its blue and white vehicles the words: Serve and Protect. However, in the black ghetcolony this slogan evokes anything but a feeling of security. Instead, it evokes a feeling of suspicion that black people are a threat to themselves as well as to the larger society and, must therefore be suppressed by rigid and often overbearing law enforcement measures. The law in America treats black people as if they have a bounty on their heads. Its main function is to quell the will of black people and project an image of authority to remind them that the violation of certain (white) sanctions/norms will be met with strong disciplinary action. Furthermore, it is a way of reminding black people that they are an oppressed people who do not respect the same kind of treatment given to others. And because the climate of the black ghetcolony ignites a certain amount of aggressive behavior, the police patrol its streets as though they were in a war zone.

A considerable amount of this patroling is spent in confrontations with youths. Black youths become the prime scapegoats of the police because they are the most defenseless and most vulnerable to the perils of trying to survive the black ghetcolony. While the dope pusher, juice dealer, fence and other criminal types are allowed to pursue their professions with little police intervention, black youths are often persecuted for even the most harmless of misdemeanors. And because they boldly display themselves on the streets and seem to be always engaged in gang wars, they become the most visible targets for the police to carry out its calculated mission. This is not to imply that black youths do not engage in a considerable amount of crime in the black ghetcolony. It would be irresponsible to make such a statement. But these crimes should not be equated with cantankerous conduct, contemptuous attitudes or even physical aggressiveness. However, often, these modes of expressions are also interpreted as being criminally oriented and subsequently those who exhibit these traits are treated as criminals. This failure to separate criminal behavior from acting-out behavior makes most black youths prone to arrest and police harassment. The Jester and the Antagonist are particularly the victims of frequent police pickups and shakedowns. This is mainly because their behavior makes them stand out; and, when police are out to make arrests, they pick up those youths who have been previously identified as deliquents. The persecution of black youths by the police creates an uncompromising situation that find members from both groups anticipating violence from the other. It is a relationship that has been strained by years of intense feelings, lack of understanding, misinterpretation of roles and the police's annual campaign to "clean-up", once and for all, those delinquent youths who create so much trouble. To the youths who live in the Street Institution the police are rarely viewed with friendly eyes. Black children learn early in life to be cautious and even disdainful of the men in blue. Perhaps, these attitudes are learned when a six-year-old boy sees his father beaten by four policemen, or when an eight-year old is caught stealing and is reprimanded as though he were a criminal. Or perhaps when a twelve-year old sees his older brother shot down by policemen, because he ran without heeding their warning to halt. And the most pathetic thing about this relationship is that few policemen do anything to improve it, but seem to expect the youths to initiate a peace treaty.

After being subjected for years to the uncontested authority of the police, black people have begun to discover that they are not treated as criminals only because of crimes they may commit, but because they are oppressed people who are subject to the first law of oppression: keep the oppressed people oppressed by denying them their fundamental liberties. It is due to this realization that crime in the black ghetcolony sometimes takes on a different interpretation, in that some acts against society are not conceived as being criminal acts but as acts of survival. However, one must be prudent in making such a distinction, for it is conceivable that some people would use it as a shield for their criminal actions, regardless of the circumstances.

THE UNIDENTIFIED CULPRIT

There is a tendency, on the part of some people, to rationalize that the black ghetcolony condones crime. This is absurd! In fact, it only indicts blacks as being lawless people. And the belief that black people have certain inherent pre-dispositions for crime is equally unfounded. Yet, many people persist in believing this myth.

"Don't go down there (black ghetcolony) after dark. You may not come out alive."

"Those people (ghetcolony dwellers) are always fighting and killing each other."

This negative image is superimposed on all those who live in the black ghetcolony and consequently an impression is created that makes no distinction among its members. And often when people are constantly identified in negative terms, they are very likely to adopt the behavior which they are accused of having.

"Well what do you expect me to do in this neighborhood, act

like a sissy?"

"Yeah man you sure gotta be bad to live around here."

Then, too, the black ghetcolony is often glamorized as being "down to earth," "nitty gritty," "where the action is," and other romantic names which give it the erroneous impression of being a poor man's paradise despite its pervasive poverty. White college students and volunteer workers, especially, like to tour its dirty streets and marvel at the colorful lifestyles, chauvinistic behavior of males and "tough looking" youths standing on corners. One group of white teachers, participating in a ghetcolony training program, got highly indignant when, during a tour of North Lawndale, they did not see "niggers fighting and drinking Ripple (wine) on every corner." Yet these same persons who romanticize the ghetcolony would become insulted if similar patterns of behavior were expressed in their communities.

Both forms of sterotyping, "bad image" and "romantic image," paint a picture of the black ghetcolony which distorts its authentic culture. And as its culture is distorted the social group which it represents is distorted as well.

Also statistics on crime in the black ghetcolony are often misleading. Usually they are compared to other communities whose crimes do not always show up on frequency charts. For instance, in white middle class communities many minor offenses are settled through station adjustments and are never formally reported. Also, there is little distinction placed between the proportion of crimes as they correspond to high density areas (black ghetcolonies) to those of low density areas (white communities).

Still we cannot easily dismiss the fact that the environmental conditions of the black ghetcolony do heighten the chances of certain types of crimes, i.e., shoplifting, mugging, robbery, burglary, etc. When powerless people are denied basic necessities and are squeezed into segregated areas which induce overcrowdedness, then it is more than probably that criminal activity will be accelerated. Regardless of those who might negate this correlation, by blaming behavioral factors rather than environmental factors as being the greatest contributor to crime, they cannot refute the disproportion of crimes that are committed in overcrowded slum communities. Frank Tannenbaum was quite aware of this cause and effect relationship as early as 1938 when he stated:

> American criminal activity must be related
> to the total social complex. The United
> States has as much crime as it generates.

> The criminals are themselves part of the
> community in its deeper sense, and are as
> much its products as are its philosophers,
> poets, inventors, businessmen and scientists,
> reformers and saints. This is a basic fact
> that we must accept. If we would change the
> amount of crime in the community, we must
> change the community. The criminal is not a
> symptom merely, he is a product, he is of
> the very bone and fiber of the community it-
> self. The community has given him not merely
> his ideals and ends, not merely his relation-
> ships with the world that make the kind of
> career he lives a possibility. The community
> has given him his methods too, whether these
> be graft, political pull, or the use of a
> machine gun. The distinction between the
> criminal and the community drawn in sharp con-
> trast—a distinction between good and evil—is
> a false distinction and obscures the issue.[1]

Although Tannenbaum does not identify one of these social complexities as racism; nevertheless, racial pathology must be seen as the greatest contributor to crime in the black ghetcolony. But of course, racism has never been a popular case for people to advocate when investigating the causes of crime; that is until the 1965 Kerner Commission Report on Civil Disorders made this view (white) official.

THE CONTROLLERS: BIG BROTHERS WITH GUNS

To maintain tight surveillance over black youths, law enforcement officials have created a number a special units. These units consist of youth officers, community relations officers and members of the controversial Gang Intelligence. Each of these units has the specific task of suppressing juvenile crime, and usually keep a file on all convicted juvenile offenders and also on those youths who are considered to be potential delinquents. Once a youth is placed on one of these lists he becomes a permanent adversary of the police. This means that whenever an offense is committed, whether it be a misdemeanor or felony, the youth is liable to be picked up and detained at the station for questioning. While this in itself may not appear to be infringing on the rights of an individual, it does allow indiscreet policemen to exercise their authority without fear of reprisal. As a result those officers who misuse this sanction can intimidate a youth at any given time and even interrogate him without due process of law. The interrogation of black youths is carried out in many subtle ways which allows the interrogator to circumvent normal law procedures. Many times a youth is held for long hours without being informed of his rights, or, for that matter, without notifying his parents or guardian. This procedure is in direct violation of a person's civil rights, but in the black ghetcolony it is administered as a "given" right. And because most black youths are not familiar with the law, a policeman can take full advantage of this ignorance and subject a youth to threats and, in many cases, physical punishment. Although youths under seventeen are supposed to be placed under the custody of youth officers or detained at the Audy Home for Juveniles, this procedure is also flagrantly violated. There are many times when juveniles are taken to the police lock-up, where they are placed with older persons, until a petition is made in the courts.

However, the greatest intimidation of black youths takes place in the streets. There they can be stopped at any time and forced to go through the degrading ceremony of being shaken down in spread eagle fashion, legs opened wide and hands braced against a wall or vehicle. This scene is so common in North Lawndale that it is done without anyone even being curious enough to watch. To a large extent, the black ghetcolony is at fault for allowing its youths to be subjected to these types of acts. But there are few adults or organizations that really seem to care how black youths are treated and consequently the police take advantage of this apathy.

POLICE BRUTALITY: A WAY OF LIFE

Although the black community has for years been making adamant accusations about police brutality, their words go unheeded. Police officials constantly deny that "Chicago's Finest" employ anything but the gentlest of methods in their dealings with youths. Yet, the number of youths who make these claims of police brutality never seems to cease. But the residents of North Lawndale have very little power to counteract these "police state" tactics. Their avenue for redress is inevitably blocked by red tape, unsympathetic police officials, inaccessibility of lawyers and the unwritten code that binds every policeman to protecting his peers from being found guilty of conduct unbecoming a police officer. But the battered faces and broken bodies of those youths who have been victimized by police cannot be hidden. They can be seen on most any corner in North Lawndale, pretending to be strong, yet knowing that their strength can be immobilized at any moment by the blunt from a policeman's club, a kick in the abdomen or a crack against the head by a revolver.

Often the most sadistic policemen are black. The psychological explanation for this is simple. The politics of oppression realize that it is necessary to include in its army of law enforcement members from the oppressed group. This form of tokenism is necessary for the oppressor to redeem itself from being labeled a racist group that takes advantage of the minority group:

> The use of the Negro as a means of con-
> trolling the Negro population at the
> level of patrolman could mean that he
> actively participates in controlling
> and containing other Negroes through
> force. It may be that from the point
> of view of the police department it is
> better to see Negro Officers actively
> containing other Negroes than white
> policemen doing the job.[2]

And some black policemen are so determined to prove their "worth" they will resort to almost anything to gain recognition from their white superiors. A black policeman who is really out to make a reputation for himself always does so at the expense of his own people.

During legalized slavery this tactic was used to help keep the slaves in order. The slavemaster would appoint other slaves, known as "drivers", to administer punishment to their peers. Lerone Bennett, Jr., describes this divisive tactic quite explicitly when he states:

> The drivers were slaves apppointed to assist
> the overseer in the field and were charged
> with keeping order in the quarters. Thorough-
> ly detested by most of their fellow bondsmen,
> the drivers were an integral part of the plan-
> tation command hierarchy. They were, in effect,
> master sargeants under a lieutenant (overseer),
> under a captain (master).[3]

Unfortunately some black policemen fall victim to this same type of divisiveness and carry out the command of their superiors with great force and enthusiasm. The black community has, historically, been plagued with more than its share of these modern day "drivers". During the late thirties, Sylvester "Two-Gun Pete" Washington acquired a most notorious reputation as a police hatchetman. "Two-Gun Pete" was known to have killed eight people, usually under questionable circumstances, and some believed that his victims numbered twice this many.

Another policeman of the "Two-Gun Pete" school is James "Gloves" Davis who was assigned in 1960 to patrol the streets of North Lawndale during the gang conflict between the Cobras and Vice Lords. "Gloves" obligingly kept the image of "Two-Gun Pete" alive and quickly established a reputation equal to that of "Two-Gun Pete", if not even more infamous. A black reporter, Francis Ward, comments on the sadistic deeds of Gloves Davis:

> James "Gloves" (Duke) Davis is a policeman
> known in the trade as a tough cop, a hatchet-
> man who is used to going in and busting up a crowd
> or rounding up a gang of "young punks" when no-
> body else will take the job. That's how he
> got the name "Gloves". For years, he earned
> his trademark by slowly, methodically slipping
> on his black leather gloves, crackling his
> knuckles, then moving in to whip some heads or
> make an arrest.[4]

James "Gloves" Davis was also one of the "hit men" who took part in the December 4, 1970 pre-dawn raid of Fred Hampton's apartment, which left Fred, the outspoken Chairman of the Illinois Chapter of the Black Panther Party, and a fellow panther, Mark Clark, dead. The controversial raid, which was engineered by State's Attorney Edward V. Hanrahan, has since come under considerable criticism, and there are many in the black community who saw it as a political execution.

Fortunately, not all black policemen become victims of their own self hate and fratricidal neuroses. In fact, most are "regular guys" just trying to do a job as best they can. But the ambivalence toward their jobs must make many of them potential schizophrenics. Having to suppress those who are being suppressed by the same system which suppresses them, undoubtedly, poses a complex situation. Nonetheless, there is a core of black policemen in Chicago, called the Afro-American Patrolman's League, who are trying to improve the image of the black policeman. Co-founded in 1968 by its present director, Renault Robinson, the AAPL has already become a formidable thorn to the politically controlled Chicago Police Department. This group has repeatedly challenged the department's ipso facto policy of discrimination and its indiscriminate suppression of the black community. The goals for this maverick organization states the following:

> 1. That the Afro-American Patrolmen's League pledge itself to the support of all community efforts devoted to establishing respect for black manhood, black womanhood and black pride within the law.

> 2. That the black community will accept and support the efforts of the Afro-American Patrolmen's League to reverse the distrust and hostility towards black police officers.

> 3. That the black community and the Afro-American Patrolmen's League dedicate themselves to the proposition that law enforcement may be practiced by black police officers with compassion, understanding and efficiency.

> 4. That the goal of law enforcement officers will become the employment of courtesy and compassion rather than the mere absence of brutality.

> 5. That the black community and the black police officers will respect the sanctity of human life whether clothed in a police uniform, a prison uniform or civilian dress.

> 6. That the black community and the black police officers will be mutually supportive of efforts to bring about a new community where unity of purpose and recognition of the nobility of the black heritage will be a deterrent to crime; where moral authority imposed from within will govern human relationships rather than technical legalism; and where those of us who are black will be able to live lives of beautiful fulfillment.[5]

Although the goals of the AAPL may appear to be rather altruistic, particularly in view of the despotic structure of the Chicago Police Department, it, nevertheless, has created considerable interest among other groups who are concerned about the poor relations between the police and the black community. The most important feature of the AAPL is that its members are trying to project a more positive image of the black policeman and establish better relations with black youth; two highly commendable goals.

PARENS PATRIAE: PROTECTOR OR SUPPRESSOR?

When youths in Chicago, sixteen and under, are arrested for an offense they are usually sent to the Cook County Family (Juvenile) Court and Arthur J. Audy Home. At times, however, the youth officer will make a station adjustment by filling out a Community Inspection Report and referring the youth to a social agency. Very seldom is a follow-up made of this type of disposition. Youths seventeen and over, when arrested, are taken to the House of Corrections or the Eleventh Street Station lock-up where they are placed with older adults, to await appearance in Criminal Court or Boys Court. Once placed in these judicial morgues, a youth has few options to protect his rights.

Chicago's Juvenile Court has the distinction of being the first such court in America, having been founded in 1899 by the Illinois State Legislature. For seventy-five years it was housed in a tangerine colored V-shaped building that stood diagonally on the corner of Roosevelt Road and Ogden Avenue. While at this location, the facilities of the Juvenile Court developed into the worst of any juvenile court in the nation, and this situation was not corrected until 1973. Now the Juvenile Court has a new building, which is located just one block away from the original one. The formation of the Cook County Juvenile Court came about because up intil 1899 children in Illinois were still being treated like criminals and subjected to the same courts and laws which presided over adults. To correct this miscarriage of justice the doctrine of *parens partiae* was adopted into law, thus giving the Family Court juridiction over offenders under the age of sixteen.

> The truly significant innovation in the
> Illinois Act was that children charged
> with law violations were not to be treat-
> ed as criminals, but were to be accorded
> the same special attention and assistance
> as dependent and neglected children. This
> is the important deviation from previous
> English and American Chancery proceedings
> involving *parens patriae* which had provid-
> ed protection only to those children whose
> distress was the result of the actions of
> their parents rather than the results of
> their own delinquent acts.[6]

However, the pioneering and laudable efforts of the Chicago Juvenile Court have failed to keep pace with the contemporary problems of youth and, today, it is understaffed, poorly supervised, assigned incompetent judges or magistrates, overtaxed with heavy case loads and operating under laws which sometimes make one wonder if a youth is not better off in a criminal court. Instead of protecting the rights of a youth as provided by *parens patriae*, the Juvenile Court has become youth's greatest antagonist. And for the black child it is like facing a kangaroo court, which is completely insensitive to the conditions that may have caused him to commit certain anti-social acts. Prior to 1930 it was other ethnic groups who made up the largest clientele at Family Court but now this is no longer true. Today, the majority of youths who appear in Juvenile Court are black. They represent a cross-section of the Street Institution: the gang member, the truant, the Antagonist, the kid with no parents or the shy youngster no one thought would harm a fly, who is faced with a charge of attempted murder. Those youths who were placed under supervision are accompanied by a parent, guardian or, perhaps, an older brother or cousin. And the youths who were detained in the Audy Home are often brought into the court building handcuffed as though they are convicted criminals.

Before adjudication is made on a youth, he has a prehearing, at which time the judge can either dismiss the charges or place the youth under court supervision and assign him a probation officer to investigate his background. These prehearings were implemented in 1968 to expedite the Court's heavy load and to filter out those youths who could be placed under supervision without being detained or required to face adjudication. If, however, the judge chooses he can detain the youth at the Audy Home or allow him to return home until the date for his adjudication hearing. At the adjudication hearing it is determined whether the youth is guilty or not and if he should be issued a delinquent petition. If the youth is given a delinquent petition he must then face a disposition hearing, at which time the court will make one of the following options:

> 1. placed on probation or conditional discharge and released to his parents, guardian or legal guardian;

> 2. placed out of his home under guardianship or custodianship of a relative or interested person with or without supervision by court staff;

> 3. committed to the Illinois Department of Children and Family Services;

> 4. committed to the Department of Corrections.

The Probational Officers of the Juvenile Courts are expected to perform herculean tasks. Some carry case loads which exceed fifty and yet they are expected to make a detailed investigation of each case, which includes the boy's family, school, peer associates and adult influences. This unreasonable expectation only means that the Probational Officer rarely gets the opportunity to make a comprehensive evaluation of a youth's background. And in court this lack of information becomes quite evident as a Probational Officer clumsily tries to state his recommendation to the judge. As a result a youth, who normally becomes non-verbal before a judge, has no one to really provide the court with pertinent sociological data and, therefore, the court seldom fully explores the circumstances which cause a youth to get into trouble. And due to their own large case loads, and impatience, most judges do not take the time to inquire about the empirical background of a boy. They simply hear the charges and in their God-like manner transfer fear to those they have the power to make judgements over. Then, too, some judges who are assigned to Family Court feel that they are the "black sheep" of the judiciary, and approach their chores with less professionalism and enthusiasm than one would expect of a magistrate.

Another bad feature of Family Court is that the legal counsels assigned to protect the rights of a youth have little time to sufficiently establish a case in behalf of the youth and usually they can be found still scanning over a youth's records seconds before court time. This is not an attack on the lawyers, many are quite dedicated, but on the system which makes it nearly impossible for them to give their clients the best legal representation.

The State's Attorney counsels are also burdened with the same problem of not having sufficient time to review cases. But their problem is more easy to overcome for most merely glance over their cases and make a plea for conviction, regardless of the evidence. State's Attorney counsels work hard to gain a conviction each time because often their professional careers are determined by the number of cases they win. They are not always interested in seeing that justice is carried out but in being able to use the court as a stepping stone for other more lucrative assignments.

A black youth only has a reasonable chance of having his rights protected in Juvenile Court when he has a private attorney. But most of these members of the bar are generally not philantropists and consequently their services do not come cheap. It is indeed a sad testimony that in this society the only difference between the innocent and guilty is usually one that depends upon one's ability to hire a good attorney.

Much has been written about the gross inadequacies of juvenile courts and the injustices they inflict on youths. Howard James was concerned about this scandalous situation and travelled throughout the country collecting data about the conditions of many juvenile courts. His comments about the Chicago Juvenile Court were anything but complimentary:

> In Chicago's huge circuit court, judges
> are usually assigned on the basis of
> preference and seniority. As could be
> expected, the juvenile court in that
> city is jammed with impossible cases
> that constantly spring from miserable
> slums and fourth-rate inner-city schools.
> Since no judge can resolve the problems
> these children face, the juvenile court
> offers hard work and little satisfaction.
> It is not a popular assignment. Often
> when a judge has been in the juvenile
> court long enough to understand the job,
> he also has enough seniority to ask for a
> transfer leaving the court filled with
> judges who know far too little about
> juvenile justice. The children in Chicago,
> as in many other cities, are more often
> harmed instead of helped by the juvenile
> court even as that city prides itself on
> establishing the first separate court for
> children.[7]

The Chicago Juvenile Court places additional stress on black youths because of its predominantly white judiciary staff. Although the present presiding judge, Honorable William Sylvester White, is black, eight of the ten calendars (court rooms) have white judges who may have little understanding of the cultural variables which cause many black youths to commit certain anti-social acts. As representatives of white middle class values, it becomes difficult for them to conceptualize the value system of the Street Institution which has played a major role in molding the behavior of delinquent black youths.

When one leaves the Juvenile Court and goes northeast on Ogden, which cuts across Chicago's mammoth west-side medical complex, he can discern many of the institutions which also help to influence the lives of black youths. There are the hospitals which bring them into the world, the clinics which treat their illnesses, the social rehabilitation schools which attempt to heal their emotional scars, the research centers which try to diagnose their problems and the Coroner's building where their deaths receive an official stamp of approval. Juvenile Court is but an appendage of this mall of institutional racism.

JUVENILE PRISONS

Youths who are assigned to the Illinois Department of Corrections are first sent to the Reception and Diagnostic Center for Boys in Joliet, Illinois. At this receiving institution, a youth is given a battery of psychological tests and has a countless number of interviews with psychologists and social workers. But these tests and interviews do little to change his situation or prepare him for confinement. On the contrary, some youths are subjected to experiments and behavior modification programs which could result in them having more serious problems at a later time. Upon leaving Joliet, a youth is sent to one of the four Juvenile Division Institutions to serve time. Needless to say, none of these institutions are designed to help him re-enter society; that is, with any sense of personal pride and development. It has been said again and again: correctional institutions rarely rehabilitate their constituents. None of the juvenile institutions in Illinois have done anything to change this dismal picture. Although the Illinois Department of Corrections calls these institutions training schools, they are operated like any adult prison for their basic philosophy is to suppress behavior rather than to develop people.

Most black youths from Chicago are sent to the Illinois State Training School for Boys in St. Charles, Illinois. Once Sheridan Correctional Center was used as a juvenile detention facility but it has now been converted to an adult institution, after a disclosure of its suppressive activities was made public by a group of concerned black citizens. However, when Sheridan was a juvenile center, it had the reputation as being the toughest and most inhumane of all juvenile institutions in Illinois. The following remarks by an ex-resident of Sheridan will give one a general picture of what this institution was actually like.

It was March 30, 1971. As I awoke this particular

> morning about 6:00 a.m., it started off like all the
> other dull mornings. I was on the East solitary con-
> finement block on the upper gallery of Building C-7.
> I had been in the "Hole" (solitary confinement) for
> perhaps a month at the time. I was in my frequent
> accustomed cell: No. 67. In Building C-7, the cells
> don't have bars like in the other security buildings.
> The cells in C-7 have solid steel doors, except for
> several "open cells" on the lower gallery. On the
> East block of the confinement cells at the bottom of
> the steel doors where there had been two inches of
> space, cells were blocked off with iron blocks, making the
> doors have a three inch slot used as an observation
> plate which slides up and down. The cells are very
> tiny, which make the inmate inside feel closed and
> boxed in; infinitely. The cells are something like
> six feet wide, nine feet long and nine feet high.
> The C-7 cells consist of: a steel desk welded onto
> the floor, a steel bed welded onto the wall, a steel
> toilet and sink combined, welded onto the floor, a
> hot pipe (heater) running from the floor to ceiling,
> and, a window with bars running across the frame
> structure.[8]

To add to these suppressive conditions, many youths were
constantly being exposed to sexual abuses, which often were
prompted by prison officials.

> When I first came here to Sheridan, I was out here
> not even a good week when a guard approached me and
> said: "...a new inmate who looks just like a little girl is
> down in the gallery." He told me that a lot of inmates
> were bugging him to let *them* in the cell with the "fresh"
> inmate - a first cop - to screw him, but since he admired
> me because: "...you don't take *no* shit," he wanted to
> let me be the first one to: "...bust through!"[9]

A youngster's ability to survive is put under the severest of tests
when he is confined to a "juvenile prison." The youth who has done
well in the Street Institution is better equipped to cope with this type
of hostile environment. However, the youth who is lacking in basic
street skills, will most likely have a very difficult time in making an
adequate adjustment. But even to those youths who have not fared
well in the Street Institution, the juvenile prison becomes an
excellent laboratory for them to make up their deficiencies. A boy is

able to learn all of the things he missed learning in the streets and will even become familiar with new lessons. Learning how to strip and steal cars, acquiring new burglary techniques, and knowing where to contact fences and dope peddlers are all rudimentary lessons which are taught in juvenile prisons. The pecking order of the Street Institution becomes the means by which youths achieve special privileges. And when the law of the Street Institution does not prevail, there is always the suppressive laws of the juvenile prison which has its own set of rewards and punishments. Those who challenge them are treated like hardened criminals and placed in solitary confinement. Sometimes the more serious violators are beaten and given amphetamines to settle them down. The Juvenile Division Institutions in Illinois are the worst examples of what a society has to offer its youths who have been branded delinquents.

Some youths in North Lawndale go in and out of correctional institutions as though they were caught in a revolving door. This high rate of recidivism can be attributed to many factors, but the most obvious one is that the conditions which contributed to their misconduct are still there when they return to the black ghetcolony. And many return with more contempt for the law and a greater knowledge of how to break it.

The prisons of Illinois are overcrowded with black men who, long before their incarceration, were destined to become outcasts of society. Many of these men were branded criminals when they were born and their early years in the Street Institution only constituted a probational period. The slightest violation of their probation automatically places them in custody and after they've served time, they are placed on parole which, for all purpose and intent, covers a life span.

For even when they are not behind bars these men are forced to live in confinement. The system which imprisons them extends beyond the walls of penal institutions and reach out into the entire black community. Every black child is a potential prisoner because of the system which continuously oppresses him.

CHAPTER NINE

EVERYBODY'S SCAPEGOAT: THE BLACK FAMILY

> We take the view that the failure to view the Negro people and particularly Negro family life from the vantage point of their own independent historicial milieu has distorted the context in which Negroes are viewed and view themselves in this society.
>
> *Black Families in White America*
> Andrew Billingsley

In 1965, the United States Department of Labor published a report which subtly vindicated white America of bearing any responsibility for the social oppression of black people. Furthermore, it took the position that the deterioration of the black community emanated from the corrosion of everybody's scapegoat, the black family. This indictment of the black family was written by one of America's elite sociologist, Daniel P. Moynihan, titled, *The Negro Family, The Case for Nation Action.* While many may feel that my reaction overdramatizes the gravity of the report, it is made not to shock but to put in proper perspective the travesty which has unjustly been placed on the black family. For in its most naked interpretation the findings documented in the Moynihan Report places the primary blame for black peoples' oppressive status in this country on the so-called instability of the black family.

> At the heart of the deterioration of
> the fabric of Negro society is the
> deterioration of the Negro family.

> It is the fundamental source of the
> weakness of the Negro community at
> the present time.[1]

This statement which serves as the basic thesis for the Moynihan Report was derived from a countless number of statistics, charts, census tracts, graphs and a few quotations, taken out of context from prominent social scientiests, a few who were black and one in particular, E. Franklin Frazier. The case which Moynihan made was clear: black people are burdened with disorganization simply because the black family has not been strong enough to rally its members to overcome the effects of slavery, poverty, caste and oppression. Although the report acknowledges the existence of these injustices and makes a few inflammatory comments about white racism it, nevertheless, maintains that a more cohesive black family unit could have made amends for these social inequities. And, of course, the inability of the black family to accomplish this "miracle" was largely due to its predominantly matriarchal structure which invariably emasculates the black male. Although this myth has been refuted many times by informed black scholars, it is still used as a rationale by mis-informed critics to interpret the hierarchy structure of the black family. In a recent study of the black family by the National Urban League, this allegation was again challenged for its authenticity.

Contrary to popular belief our findings

> indicate that most black families are
> characterized by equalitarian patterns.
> And the wives in these families, although
> strong and resourceful, are not domineer-
> ing matriarchs.[2]

While it is partially true that many black men have been unable to give their families the economic foundation desirable for family stability, their forced expulsion from the job market should not be miscontrued as to render them impotent. A close examination of the black male will reveal that he has always, to the best of his ability, provided his family with far greater support than he is normally given credit for.

What makes the Moynihan Report so detrimental to the survival of black people is that it is based on misinterpretations, maneuvering of statistics, dialectic reasoning and white mythology. And because the Moynihan Report influences many welfare programs, both public and private, its affect on the lives of black children is far reaching. For this reason, the case against the black family must be re-examined and place before a jury which is more sensitive to and better understands the unique cultural patterns of the black family.

Although some black social scientists have in the past confirmed that the black family cannot be interpreted in the same social context as the white family, because of its cultural uniqueness, the most contemporary spokesmen of this position and a staunch critic of the Moynihan Report has been Dr. Andrew Billingsley.

In his book, *Black Families in White America,* Dr. Billingsley probes deep into this uniqueness" and analyzes the black family from a sociological position, heretofore ignored. His thesis suggests that the black family must be studied as a social system, therefore, placing it in a much broader frame of reference and logical analysis:

> Four major concepts provide the essential
> elements of this perspective: (1) social
> system, (2) ethnic subsociety, (3) family
> structure, and (4) family function. Each
> of these major concepts refers to a stream
> of social science theory which has been
> developed and tested primarily in relation
> to other social phenomena than the family.
> The four are, however, highly compatible
> and suggestive for a study of Negro family
> life precisely because Negro families have
> been so conspicuously shaped by social

forces in the American environment.[3]

From this frame of reference, Dr. Billingsley divides the black family structure into three major categories, nuclear, extended and augmented, which then can be subdivided into twelve different subtypes. This analysis marks a radical departure from the traditional male dominated versus female dominated theory of families which is normally used to study family life in America. Instead, this alternative model takes into consideration the conglomerate of variables, survival techniques and cultural patterns which are acutely related to the black family.

In North Lawndale there are ample examples of each type and a glimpse into a few will reveal that they are much more stabilized than the unstable reporting of Moynihan.

THE BROWNS: A SIMPLE NUCLEAR FAMILY

Mr. and Mrs. Brown own a modest six-room bungalow with a walk-up staircase and a backyard. They have lived in North Lawndale for nearly twenty years, after having both migrated from the South. Mr. Brown is an industrious person, the prototype of the Working Man, who is fully committed to helping his family live as comfortably as they possibley can. The other members in the family include three boys, and two girls. The oldest boy recently graduated from high schol and the second oldest boy stands a good chance of going to college.

During their struggle to raise a family and pay off their mortgage, Mrs. Brown has held odd jobs at various times to give her husband as much support as possible. Her relationship to her husband is typical of the equalitarian pattern mentioned in the National Urban League's study. But her primary job has been that of a housewife although she has been active in community programs. Ever since the North Lawndale community began to undergo a sharp economic decline, she has been active in trying to improve community conditions. At one time, Mr. Brown was also active in community affairs. He once managed a little league team and did volunteer work at a social agency, but now he has become disillusioned by the lack of community pride and its rapid deterioration. Still he attempts to make the best of the situation even though he has lost some of the pioneering zeal he had when he first moved to North Lawndale.

The children all attend Catholic School and have been exposed to the rigid discipline of that religion. Nevertheless, the boys are active in the Street Institution although none have become gang members. At one time the oldest boy was a marginal delinquent but was able to escape getting into serious trouble because of the stern support of his parents. The boys have never been lacking in a father image and have been able to successfully vacillate between the Street Institution and the formal institutions without becoming confused about their roles and values.

Although the Browns would probably like to move from North Lawndale, they remain because they have built a coping foundation which has enabled family members to weather the storm of oppression. And this is fortunate for without families like the Browns, North Lawndale would have succumbed long ago.

THE ABRAMS: AN ATTENUATED EXTENDED FAMILY

The Abrams family live in one of the dilapidated two-story brick apartment buildings which are so common in Lawndale. Although the outside of the building is cluttered with debris, the five rooms which accommodate the seven members in the family are always tidy. The Abrams family consists of Mrs. Abrams, her grandmother, two boys and two girls. Not an exceptionally large family, but large enough when one takes into account that it must survive on the meager subsidy of public welfare. Mrs. Abrams has been on public assistance for at least five years and her mother, who is the strongest of the two, is a recipient of social security benefits. Mrs. Abrams and the children were all born in Chicago while the grandmother was born and raised in the South, moving to the North during the Depression of 1930.

Besides being hampered with the bureaucracy of welfare, all members of the family have, to some extent, epilepsy. Mrs. Abrams has the most serious case and has undergone a number of seizures. The oldest boy's epilepsy, though less serious, calls for him to take medication each day. The other children take periodic inspections at the hospital for preventive purposes.

Mrs. Abrams is continuously encouraging her children to get the best education possible. However, in North Lawndale this becomes rather difficult, and Mrs. Abrams makes frequent visits to the schools to insure that her children are achieving some degree of progress. The youngest boy is extremely bright but has become a behavior problem in school because his teacher fails to challenge his restlessness and finds it easier to treat him as discipline case. Mrs. Abrams is conscious of this and is constantly seeking educational alternatives which could better meet the needs of her children. Both of the girls are better than average students but the oldest boy has had a more difficult time adjusting to school. This had caused him to do poorly in school and get into conflicts with his teachers. Once he was accused of striking a teacher and, as a result was made a ward of the juvenile courts. Also, the pressure from gangs to join their ranks adds to his problems. Nevertheless, Mrs. Abrams always stands behind him although she lacks the power to change the things which make her oldest son act out.

Mrs. Abrams does have a younger brother who tries to help the family make adjustments and counsel the children when they are in trouble. The children do look up to their uncle and view him as an authority figure who has the sanction to exercise punitive measures over them. Mrs. Abrams also has a few male companions who take interest in both her and the children. While the larger society may look at these transient models with suspicion, they do provide the children with other male figures who relate closely to the family.

The remarkable thing about the Abrams family is that there does exist strong loyalties between family members and a determined resiliency to recuperate from overwhelming setbacks.

THE THOMPSONS: INCIPIENT EXTENDED AUGMENTED FAMILY

Mrs. Thompson lives with her three sons in a four room apartment which, in appearance, looks like an average middle class home. If her family did not live in North Lawndale, this analogy would have little significance. But the Thomspon family is far from being middle class, though its values are middle-class oriented, and it is only due to the perseverance of Mrs. Thompson that her home might give this impression. As the breadwinner for the family, she is not on welfare. She has been able to give her children many of the things middle class children have: decent clothes, nourishing food, adequate furniture, and some financial stability. But this has not been achieved without hard work and great sacrifice. She works long hours in a candy factory, often overtime, and has learned how to stretch a dollar to serve the family's most pressing needs. Her two older boys are in high school and the youngest is in the seventh grade.

Mrs. Thompson's challenge comes from her trying to see that her children are properly educated. Because her own formal education was terminated before she completed elementary school, Mrs. Thompson must rely fully on the schools to meet this challenge. Yet, she fulfills her role the best she can although other institutions have failed to give her additional support. The oldest boy has encountered many problems in school and, as a result, began to hang around with street gangs. Unlike his two youngest brothers, who managed to adapt to the school setting, the oldest boy was more inclined to adapt to the Street Institution. And if it were not for a concerned uncle who took time to relate to him, the oldest boy, conceivably, could have become another statistic of the juvenile court. But the boy's uncle visits the home regularly and acts as a disciplinarian whenever he is needed. His visits, undoubtedly, provide the boys with a viable image which helps them to understand things which a mother cannot explain. In fact, he is an integral member of the family unit, even though he resides elsewhere.

While some people may interpret the Thompson family as being a matriarchal unit, Mrs. Thompson is far from being a matriarch, but allows her sons to help make decisions, without pampering them or losing their respect. Of course, she is a strong woman. However, her strength is not domineering but a reflection of her determination to confront head-on the problems of raising a family in the black ghetcolony.

These family profiles, each with different family patterns, are but a few examples of how black families cope with their environment despite living in an oppressed community. This is not to say that all black families adhere to these patterns. There is a considerable amount of diversity among them. But to hold to the belief that there is widespread disruption among black families is unfounded. To some extent, the black family has had to function like a jazz combo which improvises its music according to the skills of each member. This improvisational quality of the black family has enabled it to adapt to different situations without being bound to a fixed pattern, like members of a symphony orchestra. But the central theme to this type of human orchestration has always been one of survival.

Of course, the black family leaves something to be desired, but in our modern technological society this is true of all families, even those which are middle and upper class. When the son of Sergeant Shriver, who once headed the Office of Economic Opportunity, was found smoking marijuana, Mr. Shriver did not blame this "anti-social" act on the negligence of his family, but instead blamed the "pressures of society". Yet a poor black youth caught in the same act is accused of coming from a disrupted home. What I am attempting to illustrate is that the breakdown of social order does not always start at the family level, but with the inability of institutions, social, political, and economic, to satisfactorily meet the needs of people. While the family unit should rightfully remain the foundation for the socialization of its members, it can only capably perform this task if the social systems which make up a society fulfill their tasks. And in the case of black people these social systems have blatantly ignored the needs of black families and instead subjected them to fragmented supports which are designed to collapse, regardless of how cohesive the family structure is. For years the black family has been made the scapegoat for the low social status of black people in America. It has been defiled so frequently with allegations of being inferior that it has been difficult for many to appreciate the real strengths which manifest themselves within its social structure. To label the black family as being, to paraphrase Moynihan again, "the heart of the deterioration of the fabric of Negro society," is like blaming an abandoned child for not being wanted by its parents. White America abandoned the black family when it placed black people in slavery. And from this alienation the black family has had to create its own social structures which were sculptured from a fabric already deteriorated from poverty, oppression and racism. It is time that the black family stop being blamed for the hopelessness and powerlessness that manifests itself in the black ghetcolony. Even with is shortcomings, it continues to be the one institution that has made some effort to compensate for the social malnutrition of black children. Regardless of the studies made by sociologists, anthropologists, and other theoreticians who have diagnosed the black family as being a disrupted matriarchal unit that has been severed from its original cultural heritage, the black family remains a most viable and relevant institution. If the black family were as anemic as many of its critics profess, the annihilation of black people would have been achieved long ago. What other institution has brought black people to where they are today? It would be ludicrous to credit this achievement to the irresponsible conduct of the schools, social agencies, politicians, businessmen, police or even the church.

The black family is far from being the "heart of deterioration" in the black community. If anything it is its harbinger and salvation.

CHAPTER TEN

BLACK IS BEAUTIFUL:
SELF CONCEPTS OF BLACK CHILDREN

The acceptance of the phrase "Black
Is Beautiful" is the first step in
the destruction of the old table of
the laws and the construction of
new ones, for the phrase flies in
the face of the whole ethos of the
white aesthetic.

Addison Gayle, Jr.

The streets of North Lawndale are seldom quiet.

The clamoring of black children can usually be heard, even over the blares of police sirens, fire trucks and honking automobiles. But their voices do more than compliment the pandemonium in the streets, they also dramatically describe how children see themselves and their environment.

Children are known for their bluntness.

Unlike adults they say what they actually feel. Like the round face seven year old boy who scornfully exclaims:

> "Nigger, nigger, never die,
> Black face and shiny eye,
> Crooked nose and crooked toes,
> Dat's de way de nigger goes."

Or the nine year old boy with the crooked teeth who snickers:

> "Eenie, meenie, minnie, moe,
> Catcha nigger by de toe,
> If he holla let 'm go,
> Eenie, meenie, minnie, moe."

And the remarks from older boys are equally derogatory.

> "A nigger ain't shit!"
> "Dis whole neighborhood is fucked up!"
> "Man a nigger ain't never gonna amount to nuthin!"

Black children become conscious of themselves and their environment at a very early age. Even before they reach pre-adolescence they can sense being persecuted and alienated. The signs of oppression can be clearly discerned wherever they go.

The ugliness of an overcrowded tenement with its roaches and rats does not escape their eyes.

Nor does the smell of week old garbage left piled in dirty alleys escape their noses.

Or, for that matter, neither do the caustic remarks of the administrators escape their ears.

> "They will never learn."
> "Well what do you expect from black children?"
> "Johnny, if you ever complete school, I suggest you look for a job in some factory."

Perhaps the most serious handicap derived from growing up in an oppressed environment is that a child is most likely to develop a negative concept of himself and his community. The children who live in North Lawndale generally have a poor image of both. They have become so immersed in the negative features of their community that they develop attitudes which reflect a similar form of negativism.

The black psychiatrist Dr. Alvin F. Poussaint made note of this in a speech given before the National Medical Association in 1966.

> It is well recognized that Negroes' self-concept
> is partly determined by factors associated with
> poverty and low economic class status. However,
> being a Negro has many implications for the ego
> development of young children that are not in-
> herent in lower-class membership. The Afro-
> American child develops in a color caste system
> and inevitably acquires the negative self-esteem
> that is the natural outcome of such a system.[1]

As an infant of oppression, the black child is conditioned early in life to develop certain negative attitudes about himself and his community.

His oppressor is constantly degrading his blackness as being inferior and ugly and praising whiteness as being virtuous and desirable. The motif of white America is saturated with symbols to give credibility to this racist propaganda. Snow White is a fair maiden with a face as pure as snow (if white is fair and snow is pure then what is black?), the good guys always wear white hats and even most Easter bunnies are depicted as white. While these things may appear trivial, to some, they do reflect the low value which white America has assigned to black. But even more disturbing is how white America has been cunning enough to make many black people feel responsible for their plight. This victim analysis is evidenced by those blacks who have been conditioned to first look for solutions to their problems among their own, without being critical of the social forces which create these problems and deny black people the chance to counteract them from a position of real power. For example, slum tenement residents who only blame themselves for the deplorable conditions of their buildings, without confronting the landlord who owns them and the political system which allows the landlord to violate building codes consequently, fail to conceptualize the full dimension of their situation. Another example can be illustrated in the schools. Do you simply blame the failure of public schools to properly educate students on the poor attitudes of black children or do you question the inability of the schools to develop the type of climate which is more conducive to developing the potential of each student? And is the high rate of crime in the black community a symptom of an inherent criminal tendency among black people or a reaction to the closed social system which aggravates and contributes to certain acts of hostility and aggression? When black people begin to blame only themselves for these things they ultimately become victims of self-hate, inferiority and even fratricide. Again Dr. Poussaint expounds on this problem.

> The most tragic, yet predictable part of all this is that the Negro has come to form his self-image and self concept on the basis of what white racists prescribed. Therefore, black men and women learn very quickly to hate themselves and each other because they are Negroes. And, paradoxically, black men tend to distrust and hate each other more than their white oppressor. Today, there is abundant evidence that racism has left almost irreparable scars on the psyche of Afro-Americans that burdens them with an unrelenting, painful anxiety that reaches out for a sense of identity and self-esteem.[2]

While the Street Institution is successful in teaching black children how to survive, it pitifully fails in teaching them individual and community pride. Being victims of oppression themselves, the instructors of the Street Institution have no time to teach pride, and just being able to survive one's environment does not, in itself, make one proud. Basically the Street Institution only helps one to endure his environment with less pain, but makes no effort to help a youth overcome it. As a result, the ghetcolony child finds himself in a constant battle with his own community which he views as being almost beyond salvation.

The buffer institutions, schools and social agencies, are equally negligent in providing black youths with programs which could help them develop more self pride. They are so pre-occupied with trying to control behavior and enforce rules that they have little time to help strengthen the self concepts of the children they serve. And, as has already been noted, these institutions are often the reason black children develop such poor attitudes about themselves. In recent years the public schools have increased the number of black portraits to adorn their corridors and a few have murals depicting black history. But these visual forms, though needed, cannot make a meaningful impression on a youth unless they are re-enforced by a curriculum which also emphasizes the importance of black culture and black history. Undoubtedly social agencies, especially the private ones, have greater freedom to implement black achievement programs. But they, too, seem committed to tokenism and at best only provide Afro dance lessons or maybe a class in Swahili.

In 1967, a survey was made of 120 pre-adolescents (9-12) who lived in North Lawndale to measure their racial pride and how they perceived themselves and their community, as reflected by negative and positive attitudes.[3] The survey consisted of ten questions and, before being administered to respondents, it was given twice to a random sampling of 20 other pre-adolescents to ascertain its reliability.

The results of this survey revealed the following:

Question One:	Negro is the name of a:
	a. Race *67*
	b. Nationality *32*
	c. Church Group *18*
Interpretation:	Merely reflects a lack of understanding.
Question Two:	Negroes were brought to America from:
	a. Russia *37*
	b. Africa *58*
	c. England *20*
Interpretation:	Responses show that half of the respondents either refuse to recognize their true heritage or have not been properly orientated to the history of black Americans.
Question Three:	Negroes are what color:
	a. White *2*
	b. different colors *35*
	c. Black *11*
	d. Brown *68*
Interpretation:	Responses show that respondents have mixed feelings about skin color. However, it is interesting to note that only a small percentage perceived Negroes as being black.

Question Four:	The first Negroes brought to America were:

a.   slaves *54*
b.   politicians *3*
c.   bad people *39*
d.   good people *12*

Interpretation:	Responsess show that most respondents were aware of their slave heritage although their responses to Question Two showed an insignificant indentification with Africa. Also the high percentage of responses to Letter C has definite negative implications.

Question Five:	Most Negroes are:

a.   intelligent *17*
b.   intelligent and stupid *56*
c.   stupid *33*

Interpretation:	Responses show that respondents have mixed feelings about this question. However, even though only one third responded to Letter C it becomes a significant measurement because of its obvious negative implications.

Question Six:	Most Negroes live in:

a.   poor neighborhoods *51*
b.   rich neighborhoods *4*
d.   bad neighborhoods *28*

Interpretation:	Here again respondents show mixed feelings, but it is also significant that many responded to Letter A as well as Letter D. Responses to Letter D, in particular, reflect definite negative implications.

Question Seven:	Most Negroes live in:

a.   Jackson, Mississippi *32*
b.   Denver, Colorado *3*
c.   Chicago, Illinois *68*
d.   Los Angeles, Calif. *7*

Interpretation:	Significance of response only reveal that the majority of respondents perceive Chicago as being highly populated by Negroes.
Question Eight:	In Chicago most Negroes live in:

    a.   Lawndale *38*
    b.   Old Town *12*
    c.   Hyde Park *2*
    d.   K-Town *63*

Interpretation:	Merely suggest that respondents are "turf" conscious.
Question Nine:	Most Negroes become:

    a.   good citizens *18*
    b.   bad citizens *33*
    c.   criminals *29*
    d.   doctors & lawyers *12*
    e.   boxers & janitors *22*

Interpretation:	Over two thirds of the respondents showed a definite negative attitude toward Negroes in regard to occupational achievement and citizenship conduct. Although the responses to Letter E do not necessarily reflect a negative self concept, the large percentage of responses to Letters B and C are unquestionably negative.
Question Ten:	Most Negroes are:

    a.   Catholics *26*
    b.   Methodists *35*
    c.   Baptists *29*
    d.   Moslems *12*

Interpretation:	Responses only show that respondents are representatives of major denominations and religions.

It can be concluded from this survey that the respondents, in general, have a negative attitude toward themselves and their community. Although this survey, from such a modest sampling, does have its limitations in drawing broader conclusions, one cannot easily overlook the fact that even a small percentage of the youth population in North Lawndale with such negative attitudes is distressing. And these attitudes are being developed during a period when black pride is supposed to be flourishing and "Black is Beautiful" accepted as a given.

But it is difficult for the children of North Lawndale to accept some of the platitudes of the Black Cultural Movement when they continue to be exploited and victimized by their own.

"Man dat brother with de natural sur nough pulled a sneaky deal."

"Fuck dat "Black is Beautiful" shit. Man wat I need is a gig."

"Yea, ya give de brother a black power shake and he stabs ya rite up yo ass."

Although these statements are only reactions to the movement's real meaning, it it still disheartening to see so many black youths continue to degrade its true potential. But much of this blame has to be placed upon the movement itself. The Black Cultural Movement is often alienated from the ghetcolony, despite its claim of being a movement of the people. In an article about the Black Arts Movements, I comment on this alienation.

> While the Black Arts Movement has, to a large
> extent, been successful in its appeal to young
> adults, especially students, I do have concern
> for its failure to develop functional programs
> for black children. The seeds of a viable
> esthetic must be planted during the formative
> years of a child's development, if the movement
> it to effectively serve future generations.
> Too many of our black children are still being
> subjected to white-oriented programs, such as
> Head Start, and then fed into school systems
> that are insensitive to their culture and
> which, instead, advocate institutional racism.
> Even though there is a discernable emergence of
> black awareness, many black children continue
> to suffer from inferior attitudes, stereotype
> images, negative concepts, and the lack of
> appreciation/understanding of their historical
> and cultural origin.[4]

Too often Black Nationalism spend more time mimicking the vernacular of the ghetcolony, wearing tailor made dashikis and displaying themselves as the prototypes of black manhood rather than developing and implementing functional programs which are based on deeds instead of just words. Then, too, many are so obsessed by their claim to blackness that they often are overly critical of the street instructors (pimps, hustlers, street men) who have not yet achieved the same level of awareness. Yet it is the street instructors who must be reached, first, if any appreciative impact is going to be made on the youth. But the creation of a black elite only nullifies their active participation. And few programs ever make it in the ghetcolony without being filtered through the street instructors.

Also, most black cultural groups are poorly organized and seem to rely on a wave of cosmic vibrations to carry their programs to the peope instead of communicating directly to them. And if their programs do reach the people they usually consist of romanticizing about the ancient Egyptian dynasties or the great universities which made Timbuctu the educational mecca of its day. While a knowledge of one's roots is important for developing racial pride, a child will not form a positive concept merely by exposing him to the past. Until a conscious effort is made to synthesize his past with his contemporary setting, the black child will only be able to romanticize about "Black is Beautiful" and not experience it pratically.

And though the black business community has begun to coin some of the slogans emanating from the Black Cultural Movement, there has been little effort on its part to support and finance black groups who are trying to expose black youth to a more concrete awareness of black culture and black history. The selling of Afro wigs, Afro hair products and making Santa Claus black to delight black children are all only superficial symbols which do not come close to expressing the true meaning of blackness.

If black children are to be re-directed to see themselves differently, this cannot be done by simply changing the color of certain symbols, but must begin with establishing a new set of values which can make these symbols more meaningful.

In North Lawndale there are few organizations or groups that even attempt to seriously raise the level of black consciousness among its youth. While the rhetoric of black leaders fill the air with slogans of "nation building" and "black pride," most black youths continue to live as though these catchwords apply only to a chosen few.

Black is Beautiful yes,—but the minds of black children will continue to be contaminated with doubt, hostility and negative attitudes until they can begin to achieve their true potential. The vast potential of most black children is being wasted each day. And this waste hurts not only the black community, but the larger society as well.

CHAPTER ELEVEN

TO BE YOUNG GIFTED AND BLACK:
THE POTENTIAL OF BLACK CHILDREN

> This essay is an attempt to set forth
> more clearly than has hitherto been
> done the effect which the Negro has
> had upon American life. Its thesis
> is that despite our present Negro
> problem, the American Negro is and
> has been a distinct asset to this
> country and has brought a contribution
> without which America could not have
> been; and that perhaps the essence of
> our so-called Negro problem is the
> failure to recognize this fact and to
> continue to act as though the Negro
> was what we once imagined and wanted
> to imagine him - a representative of
> a subhuman species fitted only for
> subordination.
>
> *The Gift of Black Folk*
> W. E. B. DuBois

Few children in North Lawndale ever achieve their potential. Instead their gifts and talents are destined to become lost in a gulf of poverty and oppression. Before black children become adults their future careers have already been narrowed down to menial labor jobs, going in and out of prison or, as in most cases, surviving in the Street Institution. And this society plans this destiny for them regardless of what kind of talents they might have. But the tragedy of oppressed black children is also borne, in part, by the nation which oppresses them. This relation, strange as it seems, is inevitable, for in her oppression of black children, America denies herself the fruits of their gifts and talents. And anyone who cares to dispute this fact simply has to look at what black people have already achieved in this country to dispel his doubt. These achievements have been accomplished under the most excruciating conditions and, undoubtedly, would have been surpassed many times had black people enjoyed the benefits given to the larger society. It is a fact that achievements of black people have cut across every facet of American life and have helped to make this country the world power it is today. W. E. B. DuBois, a relentless advocate of Black Pride, was quite aware of this when he stated in the forward to his book, *The Gift of Black Folk:*

> A moment's thought will easily convince
> open minded persons that the contribution
> of the Negro to American nationality as
> slave, freedman and citizen was far from
> negligible. No element in American life
> has so subtly and yet clearly woven itself
> into the warp and woof of our thinking
> and acting as the American Negro.[1]

But because of her pathological sickness (racism), white America refuses to acknowledge this legacy and prefers to destroy young black talent each day under the name of Holy Mary, the constitution, social welfare, law and order, Yankee Doodle Dandy and apple pie. It would be impossible to even begin to speculate the countless number of black children who, if they received the opportunity, could make outstanding contributions to this country as well as to the rest of the world. Instead the gifts and talents of black children are wasted in America's ghetcolonies and bring about an irrevocable loss to mankind. There is no telling what the children of North Lawndale could achieve if this society would give them a chance and show them some love and consideration.

JOHNNY

One case in point is Johnny who belongs to Lawndale's second generation of black youths. His parents moved there during World War II. Johnny was a habitual truant when he was eight years old and spend most of his time in the streets, probing his environment and searching for explanations which no one could give him. He was deeply curious, yet his thin, rigid face made him appear dull and listless. Often he was hungry. It was difficult for his parents (his father is semi-invalid) to properly feed nine children on an income of less than three hundred dollars a month. So Johnny learned to feed himself from candy bars he would steal from the corner drug store. On the few days he did attend school, his teacher constantly reprimanded him, and Johnny quickly withdrew into his protective shelter of silence. Once he placed second in his school's annual inventor's contest with his entry of a model airplane which could play music when flying. But his second place certificate was eventually evoked, for some of the school officials couldn't accept the fact that the unique plane was Johnny's creation. This greatly distrubed Johnny and he stayed away from school the remainder of the semester. Johnny did not enter high school until he was sixteen years old. Most of his teachers thought he was "stupid". But in the Street Institution he was respected for his skill in electricity. Johnny was able to repair most radios and could even fix some televisions. His enthusiasm for repairing things was also the reason he was sent to St. Charles training school. He was sent there after he had broken into a television shop and stolen over three hundren dollars in merchandise, none of which was ever retrieved. The judge took little time to make his decision.

At St. Charles, Johnny was unable to pursue his real interest, but he did learn how to become a better burglar. Today he is a two-time loser. Yet, he had the potential to become an electrical engineer.

RALPH

And there is Ralph, who, at the age of eight, was a pudgy youth who seemed to be at odds with the world. By the time he reached thirteen he had already established a reputation in North Lawndale as being one of its most cantankerous youths. He consistently went in and out of juvenile court and when he had reached fifteen had spent over twenty-six months in correctional institutions. No one was successful in establishing a meaningful relationship with him. His father gave up when Ralph was seven years old and his mother was too occupied trying to raise the other eight children to respond to his needs. Ralph's closest companion was a youth five years his senior who was the war counselor of a street gang. Ralph looked up to him and would do almost anything he asked. But when Ralph was not getting into trouble he could be found playing a musical instrument, whenever he could steal or borrow one. He taught himself to play the clarinet, trumpet, saxophone and could do fairly well on the piano. Ralph could also compose music. He even wrote a few compositions for a local combo. And once he was a member of his high school band but was expelled because he struck another member across the head with a trumpet. No one took an interest in Ralph after that and there were no other institutions, it seemed, to assist Ralph in further developing his talent for music. Ralph is now serving a five to twenty-year sentence for aggravated assault and attempted murder at Pontiac Prison. Ralph could have become an outstanding composer or famous musician, but he won't.

JAMES

And there is James who, when in the fifth grade, scored 150 on the IQ test. He was extremely bright and when he entered high school continued to excel in his studies. But James also possessed a marvelous physique which quickly drew the attention of the football coach. At first he wasn't too enthusiastic about football. He wanted to become a lawyer, but the coach was able to persuade him to come out for the team. In his sophomore year, James did well in football though his grades did drop somewhat. However, during a practice game the following season, he suffered a broken leg and was forced to miss the whole semester. James's leg never healed satisfactorily. His family could not afford better medical treatment, and the school did nothing to help after the insurance had expired..

Upon release from the hospital, James decided to get a job to help his family and save a little money for the time when he would return to school. But after searching for seven months. James became frustrated and eventually found himself becoming an active member of the Street Institution. It took him no time to become the leader of one of the largest gangs in K-town. His intelligence and physical statue made him a ideal leader and before long his group had established a wide reputation. During this period no one made a serious effort to inquire into why James had not returned to school or made an attempt to re-direct his intelligence to pursue other goals.

And as his gang grew so did their encounters with the police. James had managed to avoid direct confrontation with the police, although he had been marked as one of their prime targets. Then he began taking drugs, perhaps from disillusionment over not returning to school or just plain frustration. At the age of eighteen he was an addict. And two days after his twenty-first birthday James was killed by a policeman during an alleged hold-up. James might have become a judge someday, but the obstacles in his life were too much for him to overcome.

There are many Ralphs', James', and Johnnies' in North Lawndale. They are everywhere, lagging pennies on sidewalks, throwing rocks at school windows, playing softball in the streets, hanging on street corners or stealing tires from a car. But most people fail to see the gifts and talents they possess and subsequently the Street Institution and the other formal institutions do nothing to prepare them to become anything other than frustrated and embittered adults. Often the expectation for achievement in the black ghetcolony mirrors its own state of hopelessness. Black children are not really expected to achieve, only to survive. Their aspirations are usually relegated to gaining a reputation in the streets. Because of this low level of expectation, few black children ever envision themselves becoming atomic energy experts, ambassadors, senators, electrical engineers or psychiatrists. But many do think of becoming hustlers, pimps and street men. And, as one would expect, the administrators do very little to encourage them to think otherwise. In fact, the administrators assume the explicit responsibility for regulating the number of black children who do show promise. In this manner they can control the number of children who will be allowed to rise above their environment and, at the same time, brainwash this minority to become their fellow conspirators.

Another factor which impedes the potential of black children from being realized is that the symbols for success in this society are created for whites and correspond to their system of values. Consequently, the black child finds himself being measured by white standards and is unable to appreciate his own talents which are developed from a different set of values. Values such as having a college education, ownership of property and financial assets are not easily obtained by blacks and, as a result, only frustrate those who pursue them. There are few success symbols created by blacks to give recognition to their own. Even those who have managed to obtain some status usually do so with the blessings of white America. In fact, the major criteria for achievement (pulitzer prize, outstanding men, who's who in America, etc.) come from standards established by whites. And even when black people parrot white values they take an inferior position within the social order of the larger society.

Since the Street Institution is viewed as an illegitimate social system, its values are denounced by the larger society and labeled as being anti-everything which does not conform to the norms of the larger society. Therefore, those who subscribe to its values are seen as social deviants. Yet despite the stigma assigned to them there is a wealth of talent among black children. But their true gifts remain submerged because they are unable to penetrate the wall of oppression which keeps them from achieving their true potentials.

When the late black playwright Lorraine Hansbury wrote her poignant play, "To Be Young Gifted and Black," she was also writing the biographies of thousands of black children. The title of her play was later composed into a beautiful song by the high priestess of black music, Miss Nina Simone. The song attempts to inspire black children to realize their own true talents.

> Young, gifted and black
> Oh, what a lovely, precious dream,
> To be young, gifted and black
> Open your heart to what I mean.

In these lines Miss Simone sets the tone for her inspirational message and invites black children to probe into their hearts, to recognize that this is true. She continues to say:

> In the whole world, you know,
> there's a million boys and girls
> Who are young, gifted and black;
> And that's a fact!

Here Miss Simone reaches out to the whole black world, not just in North Lawndale, Harlem and Watts but to Johannesburg, Jamaica, West Indies, Camora Laye, Guinea and everywhere else where black children live. And she leaves little doubt that being gifted and black is something very special.

> To be Young, gifted and black
> Is where it's at!
> Is where it's at!
> Is where it's at!

The lyrics to "To Be Young Gifted and Black" are lyrics all black children must come to believe in. They must begin to see themselves as beautiful and gifted people. But of course no song, no matter how inspirational, can compensate for the real needs of black children.

It cannot provide a child with an education after he has been kicked out of school.

It cannot provide a child with a decent home when he must share a four room tenement with ten other brothers and sisters.

It cannot change the racist institutions which vent their hate on him.

It cannot remove the hustlers, pimps, and street men who are his adult models.

It cannot prevent members from street gangs from intimidating him for not joining their ranks.

And it cannot remove a bullet from his head that comes from the gun of an irate policeman.

These things will only be abolished when the black community is able to provide its children with new alternatives which can help them overcome their oppression. It should be evident by now that the majority of black children will never achieve their potential under the present social system which strangles their development. Though America has great resources and stands as one of the world's most powerful nations, she stubbornly refuses to yield to the needs of black people. The black community can ill afford to wait until white America decides, if ever, to give black people their share of the American Dream. If the children of North Lawndale and other black ghetcolonies throughout this country are to ever develop their potentials, there must be a radical reordering of institutions and priorities in their environment.

What exists today in North Lawndale is the antithesis of what we must begin to offer black children. We can no longer think only of how to help them survive, but more crucial how to help them begin to live as free human beings.

CHAPTER TWELVE

BEYOND SURVIVAL:
FORMATION OF ALTERNATIVE INSTITUTIONS

All these institutions will be
alternatives to the Euro-American
or Negro institutions that exist,
but will exist in their own right
as expressions of the Black sensibility and
not merely as reactions to an alien sensibility.

Imamu Amiri Baraka

As influential as the Street Institution is in helping black children to cope with a system of oppression, it must be abolished. The streets of North Lawndale serve only as survival arteries but do not help a child to go beyond their closed boundaries. Instead they just take a child through an obstacle course which never ends until his death. The function of the Street Institution is to help children cope with oppression but not to overcome it. In fact, its very existence is counter to any movement that seeks to gain total liberation for black people. Though it stands as a necessary interim for survival, it fails to prepare a child for higher goals. The Street Institution is a product of oppression and as such can only operate as an artificial panacea. It cannot help black children plan for the future because it is so immersed in the daily struggle of survival. It cannot muster an offensive because it is constantly being put on the defensive. The Street Institution recognizes oppression, accepts it, and then develops a coping posture to survive in spite of it.

However, making it in the streets does not mean one will make it in the world. The streets are only a microcosm of a much larger universe and those who will survive in the end must learn to act on its stage. We must cease this romanticizing about how much soul it takes to live in the ghetcolony. So long as we teach black children that surviving in the ghetcolony is a virtue, they will never become motivated to seek out new alternatives which can help change it. Nothing would please our oppressors more than to have black children feel that surviving in the ghetcolony is equivalent to victory. An accomplishment yes—but by no stretch of the imagination can we ever begin to accept survival in place of freedom. Black children must be taught that their world extends beyond the boundaries of the ghetcolony, and that remedies for improving it will never be found in soul talk, street posturing, superfly styles or experiments with drugs.

The black child must be given an opportunity to live as a free human being. To only prepare him to survive today is to negate his chances for living tomorrow. To merely make accommodations in his environment is like telling him that he will always have a fragmented life. And to only teach him how to survive is to deny him those skills which could help him to gain control over his destiny. The maintenance of survival skills should no longer be a priority for black people. As a people we have already survived some four hundred years without gaining full freedom. Death comes to everyone and no survival program can alter this reality. But it is possible to affect the manner in which people live by building institutions which provide them with more humanistic alternatives.

If we are to ever fully realize the talents of black children, we must develop alternative structures which will help them rise above their environment. These new institutions must teach a child more than just how to survive (though they cannot exclude the teaching of survival skills) but how to take command of himself and begin to strengthen his community through positive actions. And these new institutions must be seen as more than "life preservers" to carry a child through another day. They must be systematically woven into every fibre in the black community to weave a collective garment which can bring all black people closer together. The goal of alternative institutions must be committed toward the making of a new black child, one free from identity conflict, self persecution, negative identification and the feeling of hopelessness. This, of course, will be difficult. The Street Institution is so firmly entrenched in the ghetcolony that it will take major surgery to change it. Yet, new institutions will not appreciatively affect the lives of black children by operating in a vacuum. They must be structured to influence a child's total environment. In many ways, this structure should be similar to the institutions which exist in many Afrikan societies.

In most Afrikan societies the transition from adolescence to adulthood is marked by well-defined rituals and organized social processes which fulfill the aspirations of a group's particular value system and culture. It is a period of orderly maturation that allows a youth to develop his true potential in accordance with the role expectations a society prescribes for its members. The Afrikan youth enters adulthood with a full understanding of his responsibility to his community and a knowledge of his functionary role as a member of his community. But equally important, it is a period that reaffirms the functions of each institution in his community which helps to shape and contriubute to his well-being. This initiation process is usually called the Poro and it is considered to be the most important period in a youth's development. The Afrikan community takes great pain to insure that each child born into its culture receives the maximum support, love and guidance.

> Every child is a treasured element of
> the society irrespective of how it was
> conceived. Once it has been born a
> child is an accepted commodity, and the
> Ghanaian in his right senses with his
> feet firmly fixed in his traditions will
> do all possible to see that it grows in
> happiness.[1]

The Afrikan proverb "Children Are The Reward of Life" has real significance in Afrikan societies, for these societies realize that true "nation building" depends upon how successful they are in molding the lives of their children. Therefore, Afrikan societies make sure that each of their institutions is organized in such a manner that a youth learns to live in harmony with the values and traditions which help to maintain and perpetuate the culture of their communities.

If alternative institutions are to have a similar influence on black youths in the ghetcolony, they first must have an alternative value system to give them direction and purpose.

BLACK VALUE SYSTEM

The way people live is generally determined by the value system to which they are exposed. Maulana Ron Karenga, a black nationalist and founder of the US organization, is a strong advocate of this belief and, in his efforts to re-direct black people to adopt positive goals, he has written a black value system called the Nguzo Saba. The Nguzo Saba is based on the customs and traditions of Afrikan societies and is as Karenga states, "a weapon, a shield, and a pillow of peace." The Nguzo Saba consists of seven principles which embrace both spiritual and scientific concepts.:

> Umoja (Unity) - to strive for and maintain unity in the family, community, nation and race.
>
> Kujichagulia (Self Determination) - to define ourselves, name ourselves, and speak for ourselves, instead of being defined, and spoken for by others.
>
> Ujima (Collective Work and Responsibility) - to build and maintain our community together and to make our brothers' and sisters' problems our problems and to solve them together.
>
> Nia (Purpose) - to make as our collective vocation the building and developing of our community in order to restore our people to their traditional greatness.
>
> Kuumba (Creativity) - to do always as much as we can, in the way we can in order to leave our community more beautiful and beneficial than when we inherited it.
>
> Imani (Faith) - to believe with all our heart in our parents, our teachers, our leaders, our people and the righteousness and victory of our struggle.

Although all black people do not prescribe to Karenga's doctrine, the Nguzo Saba is, at least, an attempt to establish a way of life which differs from the Euro-American sensibility that has enslaved black people over the years. For black people to deny the need for an alternative value system is to disclaim the fact that they are oppressed. Black people are still treated as slaves because of a white value system which fails to recognize them as human beings. To continue to support this system would be to condone the values which foster racism and oppression. Regardless of what value system black people adopt, it should be unequivocally clear that the system must be opposed to the one which currently keeps them in a condition of neo-slavery.

The building of alternative institutions should begin in the area of education. Since the public school is so instrumental in exposing black children to the dogma, propaganda and mythology of white racism, it should be the first to be replaced. The black child must not wait until he reaches adulthood before he is exposed to new alternatives. His orientation to them should take place during his formative years and not as a latent reaction to the indoctrination of white racism.

Alternative schools have been established in various cities throughout America. These schools are being developed on the assumptions that (1) black children cannot achieve their potential in the formal school, (2) a people struggling to liberate themselves cannot rely on the resources of their oppressor and (3) public schools are only assisting in the early destruction of black children.

In 1970, a Workshop on the Independent Black Institution was held at Nairobi College in Palo Alto, California to establish guidelines, formulate goals and make assessments of the programs which have emanated from these fledgling institutions. The following recommendations emerged from this workshop and are used as the working ideology for the development of a black institution:

(1)   recognition of what the educational process is or should be, a process which prepares people to fit into a society and serve that society, particularly in relation to the survival of the society and the individual;

(2)   recognition of the contemporary social, political, economic and educational context in which Black Americans must function and recognition that racism is a pervasive phenomenon within and throughout American social institutions;

(3)   recognition that the Black American is functionally

ignorant, that is, he is either "over educated" (educated to serve a society too technically advanced for the needs of our people) or "mis-educated" (not educated for community development);

(4) recognition that poverty and social evils do not come about because of laziness, unemployment, and poor education, but rather result from an economic system designed to maintain poverty;

(5) recognition that traditional solutions to the "Black Problem" (eg., integration) have not been functionally appropriate;

(6) recognition that the concept of independence implies the building of an independent society through the development of independent social institutions—which by necessity involves the acquisition of land and power through struggle, revolution, and, if necessary war.[2]

And in June of 1970 another conference, aimed to define new black institutions, was held in New York City. Composed of independent schools from six different cities it came to be known as the Federation of Pan-African Educational Institutions. In the words of its chairman, Leon Moor, the purpose of this alternative system "is to institute a system of independent, Pan-African education from the cradle to the grave."

North Lawndale does have one alternative school that models itself from the principles of Pan Afrikan education. The Shule Ya Watoto (School for Children) is located at 3324 West Roosevelt Road in a facility provided by the Lawndale Peoples Planning and Action Conference. Its founder is Hannibal Afrik Tirus (Harold Charles), a dedicated teacher who teaches biology at Farragut High School. The Shule Ya Watoto is part of the Afrikan Peoples Union, an organization which practices the Nguzo Saba and Pan Afrikanism. The school serves youths from ages three to sixteen and is staffed with volunteers. Although it operates only on Saturdays, it does provide black youths with an alternative that is more consistent with the goals of a meaningful and liberating educational experience. The curriculum for the Shule Ya Watoto is divided into two major categories, academic reinforcement and character development.

CONCEPT OF ACADEMIC REINFORCEMENT

Within the academic sector, we provide classes in Somo (reading), Hesabu (mathematics), Maarifa Ya Vitu Vyote (natural science) and our language arts is centered around Kiswahili.

A. *Somo* [*reading*]

The objectives are to enable students to recognize vowels and consonants, separate words into syllables, increase vocabulary by word recognition and interpreting the meaning of short essays or stories.

Materials used are geared for the age level and reading proficiency of each student as much as possible. Frequently, reading resources used are relevant magazines, periodicals, newspapers of teacher-reproduced materials.

Each child participates in a 30-minute class.

B. *Hesabu* [*mathematics*]

The objectives are to enable students to perform basic skills in adding, multiplication, subtraction and division. The most common method used is repetitive drill after a pre-test is administered to identify where the major weaknesses exist.

Once the basic manipulations are understood, problem-solving with decimals, fractions, exponents, etc. is introduced. Introduction in algebra is provided for students when they are ready.

Each child participates in a 30-minute class.

C. *Maarifa Ya Vitu Vyote* [*natural science*]

The objectives are to enable the student to better appreciate the environment, increase knowledge of living matter and become exposed to the problem-solving activity of scientific investigation.

Maximum use of student laboratory projects is emphasized including activities of growing plants, watching animal development, recording experimental data and interpreting results. Many of the projects are kept by the students for further explorations at home. The use of outdoor environment is encouraged by nature walks and research.

Each child participates in a 30-minute class and uses any extra time for keeping notes and maintenance of their project.

D. *Kiswahili*

The objectives are to introduce another language form to promote reading, writing and oral expression, as well as to develop self-confidence through success in speaking with another vocabulary.

Primarily, this native East Afrikan language is incorporated throughout the SHULE curriculum since it is the language form that is used in rituals, greetings, titles, counting, ceremonies, etc.

A group class is conducted at the beginning of the SHULE day in which specific assignments are reviewed and new vocabulary introduced. Individual and group recitations promote success in learning.

CONCEPT OF CHARACTER DEVELOPMENT

In order to produce a well-rounded Afrikan student, learning experiences must be provided for building integrity, confidence, cooperation and respect for the family, community, and Nation. The SHULE strives to achieve these goals by providing instruction in Utu Uzima (Black Manhood), Utu Uke (Black Womanhood), Self-defense, Sewing and dancing, as well as Kuumba (creativity) through arts and crafts.

A. *Utu Uzima [Black Manhood]*

The objectives are to enable the students to internalize qualities of a strong Black man and display these qualities through practical application. Young warriors are taught to become providers, protectors and develop the flexibility to adjust easily and accept responsibility for educating younger warriors.

Classes emphasize strength through self-discipline, and obedience as well as learning concrete skills in first-aid, camping and survival techniques and personal hygiene.

B. *Utu Uke [Black Womanhood]*

The objectives are to enable the students to internalize qualities of an efficient Black queen and display these through practical application. Young sisters are taught their roles in order to 1. inspire warriors to be strong, 2. educate children in the home, 3. provide social development for the Nation.

Classes emphasize correct behavior through self-discipline and obedience as well as learning concrete skills in nutrition. homemaking, arts and personal hygiene.

All queens participate in the 30-minute class.

C. *Self-Defense*

The objectives are to enable the students to respect their bodies, strengthen their minds and acquire skills in martial arts for self-defense.

Emphasis is placed on self-discipline and obedience so that instruction is balanced with physical and mental development. Presently students are learning Karate and instruction is provided for students capable of attention to details. These students receive two hours of instruction.

D. *Sewing and Dancing*

The objectives are to enable students to discipline their hands, minds and bodies toward a completed project. In sewing, manual dexterity is stressed and many items are placed on sale in the Parent Council Zawadi (gift) shop.

Through dancing, rhythmic movements are coordinated into group harmony and cooperation. The outcome of this activity is displayed through public performances. These students receive two hours of instruction.

E. *Kuumba* [*Creative Arts*]

The objectives are to enable students to develop their creative skills through coloring, painting, drama, wood sculpture and still photography. Many of the finished projects are either placed on display or on sale.

Of course, it would be premature to expect that alternative institutions will, at this time in history, serve the majority of black children. They are too few and most are still in their embryonic stages and have yet to develop the resources needed to reach large numbers of children. Then, too, there are the problems of insufficient funds which prevent them from expanding as well as the fact that many black people remain skeptical of their ability to compete with the public schools. The majority of black people still have some faith in America and feel that this country will ultimately respond to their needs. The system of oppression, with all its dehumanizing effects, has been quite successful in brainwashing many black people to believe that beneath its exploitive tactics lies a humanitarian concern for their welfare. This guise of latent self-righteousness makes it very difficult for oppressed people to lose complete faith in their oppressors and, because of this guarded optimism, seem willing to wait for this system to vindicate itself. Therefore, alternative institutions will have to demonstrate, beyond any doubt, that they are the only viable means by which black people will be able to counteract the negative teachings of traditional institutions.

At present, alternative institutions for black people will only serve as models which, if they prove to be successful over a long period, will gain greater support from the black community. But until that time comes, efforts must continue to reach the millions of black children who find themselves locked in traditional institutions. This means that those people who sincerely want to help black children must do everything possible to alter these institutions from within. So long as some black children are forced to endure these oppressive structures, concerned black administrators must remain in them. Social advocates who teach in public school and work in the various private and social agencies must disengage themselves from bureaucratic traditions and seek to develop new and creative ways of working with oppressed black youths. Paulette Jones, a graduate student at Governor's State University, Park Forest, Illinois, provides an excellent description of what this "new system" should be like.

> The new system will require that "authorities"
> develop new attitudes and behaviors as opposed
> to being confined to the behaviors limited to
> counselors, social workers, probation officers,
> teachers, etc. Many "authorities" "swear" by
> their job descriptions, and may never reach
> beyond those limits. The new system may require other
> labels to help negate the stereotypes produced by the pre-
> sent antiquated system. For example, the new
> system may 'call' counselors and/or probation
> officers Youth Advocates and a youth advocate
> need not be limited to "what-has-been-done-before."
> As an advocate for youth, he may logically do any-
> thing that promotes the development of potential.
> There is no reason why a probation officer or a
> school counselor cannot be an advocate for youth
> (the connotations are different, and negative
> assumptions are removed). Certainly, the present
> behavior-limiting labels and stereotypes do not
> help a counselor, a probation officer, a social
> worker, etc. do the "job" any better. Besides,
> the conceptual image of the old labels, held by
> Black youth, does not help the relationships that
> need to be established. In changing the labels
> for the 'new authorities', it may be meaningless
> to continue calling a youth that has had problems

with school officials or the courts a "delinquent."
Another term which will broaden the scope of the
youth's existence, connote more positive images
of himself, and even assume some of the
'special' cultural norms would provide the
impetus and avenues for positive change,
workable solutions, and declining statistics.

This "new system" must also develop "Street Therapists" who are trained to venture out into the streets and relate directly to the instructors of the Street Institution.[4] This will be no simple task but we cannot expect black youths to change without affecting the self-defeating and self-destructing lifestyles of the street instructors. These Street Therapists must be prepared to go into taverns, pool halls and linger on the corners where most street instructors congregate. Traditional social agencies have completely ignored the streets and, instead, most of their workers are confined to building-centered programs. The priorities of social agencies must shift to include providing direct services to the men in the black ghetcolony. They must develop viable street programs that are able to penetrate the very life of the Street Institution, the street instructors. One way of reaching the street instructors could be through storefront centers which would offer them a range of meaningful programs. These centers would be staffed not only with Street Therapists but also with job counselors, doctors, lawyers, and other social advocates. I'm under no illusion that such centers would change the lifestyles of all the street instructors. However, they might just perhaps help a few of them to see the futility of their existence and become motivated to seek more positive and productive lives.

North Lawndale has yet to frame an alternative way of life for its black children. The Street Institution still looms as the most formidable force in their lives. But it is imperative that it be dismantled if the children of North Lawndale are to be spared from further destruction. Somehow North Lawndale must begin to see the futility of its existence and question whether it will ever become free under the oppressive social system which now serves as its umbilical cord.

Regardless of how much faith black people still have in the American system, their ultimate liberation will only come about as a result of their own advocacy and sacrifice. This does not mean that the full burden for community improvement should be lifted from those who are in power. The main responsibility for rehabilitating North Lawndale still rest with those who control and manage the wealth in this country. It does mean, however, that those who are oppressed must, first, mobilize their own resources before they can be strong enough to demand (or take, if necessary) what they need. Oppression will never be severed by those who foster it but only when the oppressed are able to mount sufficient resources to contest it. Although the resources in North Lawndale appear limited in comparison to the awesome strength of those who hold the power in Chicago, they can be made more effective when put into maximum use. But before this can happen there must be greater community unity and consensus concerning priorities. Group divisiveness still remains one of the oppressor's best means to maintain oppression. Organizations, in particular, must stop exploiting youth for their own vested interests and began to realize that the preservation of youth is the only way a people can ever expect to sustain themselves.

North Lawndale must never cease its advocacy but, instead, increase it to such heights that even the mute ears of white America might finally awaken to the reality that the survival of the oppressor is extricably linked to the survival of the oppressed.

The children of North Lawndale will remain victims of oppression until there is a radical change in their environment. A change which offers them something more than paternalistic social agencies, street gangs and negative adult models. The streets of North Lawndale could become a meaningful home for these oppressed children if they were repaved with resourceful institutions which were committed to improving their welfare. As they exist today, these concrete arteries are only blocks which can only lead black children to further destruction.

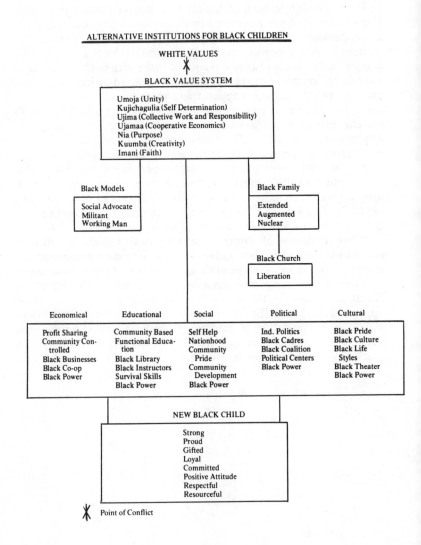

ALTERNATIVE INSTITUTIONS FOR BLACK CHILDREN

WHITE VALUES
✗
BLACK VALUE SYSTEM

Umoja (Unity)
Kujichagulia (Self Determination)
Ujima (Collective Work and Responsibility)
Ujamaa (Cooperative Economics)
Nia (Purpose)
Kuumba (Creativity)
Imani (Faith)

Black Models

Social Advocate
Militant
Working Man

Black Family

Extended
Augmented
Nuclear

Black Church

Liberation

Economical	Educational	Social	Political	Cultural
Profit Sharing	Community Based	Self Help	Ind. Politics	Black Pride
Community Con-	Functional Educa-	Nationhood	Black Cadres	Black Culture
trolled	tion	Community	Black Coalition	Black Life
Black Businesses	Black Library	Pride	Political Centers	Styles
Black Co-op	Black Instructors	Community	Black Power	Black Theater
Black Power	Survival Skills	Development		Black Power
	Black Power	Black Power		

NEW BLACK CHILD

Strong
Proud
Gifted
Loyal
Committed
Positive Attitude
Respectful
Resourceful

✗   Point of Conflict

EPILOGUE

THE NEW BLACK CHILD

the new Black Child
be he from North Lawndale, Harlem or Watts
will have a broader vision
a kinship with Africa
an awareness of his people

he will know who he is
where he came from
and what he must do

he will know Emmett Till, Michael and John Soto
Milton Olive, Jr., Mark Moore, James Johnson,
James Featherstone, Fred Hampton, Mark Clark,
James Satterfield and Ruwa Chiri

and will know why they died
and what they died for

and will obligingly
follow their paths
without fear
or intimidation
his eyes clear
sharply focused
on positive images

not on pimps, hustlers and street men trying to
steal another second to live another minute

but on black men who stand like men because they
are real men

he will join a gang
but one that protects the community
and cleans it of dirty streets/corrupt politicians/
dope/rip-off artists/and con men/

and will help gang members
understand that fratricide is genocide
and that you don't "own a turf"
just because you walk on it
but only when you control
it with your own Black Power

and he will learn
study hard and diligently
his big eyes beaming with enthusiasm
to become what he
is capable of being

but he will also help those in need
the junkie/derelict/alcoholic/prostitute/wino/
and the old man whose dreams have been absorbed
by years of frustration

and he will have respect
for his family/his father/mother/sister/brother
cousin/uncle/and aunt/
help it to grow strong

(stronger than Moynihan's family)

and he will not call his brothers
a negro/muthafucker or even a   (nigger)

and he will
defend his right
to be a man
a real man

not a john wayne/humphrey bogart/OO7/superman/tarzan/
or snow white's shining prince/

and he will protect
his community from
irate policemen
benevolent misfits/
social technicians/
bureaucratic freaks/
frustrated cynics/

and confirmed racists/

he will be
the silhouette of Africa
the harbinger of hope
the son of Allah

with the strength of Paul Robeson
the wisdom of W. E. B. DuBois
the commitment of Sekou Toure
the leadership of Kwame Nkrumah

the spirit ot Malcolm X
the charisma of Dr. Martin Luther King
the courage of Patrice Lumumba

he will be the profile of Blackness

he's coming
he's coming

look out white America
look out white America

the new Black Child is coming.

BIBLIOGRAPHY

CHAPTER ONE

1. Chicago Urban League Research Report, *Negroes in Policy-Making Positions in Chicago* (Chicago: Chicago Urban League, 1968), p. 1.

2. Ibid., p. 13.

3. City of Chicago Department of Development and Planning, *Mid-West Development Area,* March, 1957, p. 10.

CHAPTER THREE

1. This point of view was expressed by Dr. Orlando L. Taylor in his lecture titled, "Black Language in the Urban Settling" at the Schwab Rehabilitation Hospital in Chicago, Illinois, on June 15, 1971.

2. Howard E. Seals, *You Ain't Thuh Man Yuh Mama Wuz,* (Chicago Self-Published Pamphlet), (1969), p. 3.

3. Rodger D. Abrahams, *Deep Down in the Jungle,* (Hatboro, Penn., Folklore Associates, 1964), p. 57.

4. Ibid., p. 58.

CHAPTER FOUR

1. Frederic M. Thrasher, *The Gang* (Chicago: University of Chicago Press, 1968, p. 132.

2. E. Franklin Frazier, *The Negro Family in the United States,* (Chicago: University of Chicago Press, 1939), p. 277.

3. Chicago Commission on Race Relations, *The Negro in Chicago,* (Chicago: University of Chicago Press, 1922), p. 12.

4. St. Clair Drake and Horace R. Clayton, *Black Metropolis,* (New York: Harper and Row, 1945), p. 202.

5. Earl Doty, "New Dimensions of Street Work," *Viewpoint,* (YMCA of Metropolitan Chicago, Third Quarter, 1968), p. 8.

6. Ibid, p. 9.

7. Citizens' Committee To Study Police-Community Relations, *Police and Public: A Critique and A Program* (Chicago: Citizen's Committee, 1967), p. 95.

8. Statement made by undisclosed community organizer in 1971.

9. Self-published pamphlet circulated by "Teen Nations" and the Black Panther Party (1967).

CHAPTER FIVE

1. Paulo Freire, *Pedagogy of the Oppressed* (New York: Seabury Press, 1973), p. 55.

2. Harlem Youth Opportunities Unlimited, Inc., *Youth In The Ghetto,* (New York: HARYOU 1964), p. 11.

3. Malcolm X with the assistance of Alex Haley, *The Autobiography of Malcolm X* (New York: Grove Press, 1964), p. 386.

4. Iceberg Slim, *Pimp, The Story of My Life.*

5. Anita Monte and Gerald Leinwand, *Riots,* (New York: Washington Square Press, 1970), p. 19.

6. Charles V. Hamilton, "Riots, Revolts and Relevant Response" in *Black Power Revolts,* ed: Floyd B. Barbour (Boston, Mass: Porter Sargent Publisher, 1968), p. 174.

7. Richard Wright, *White Man Listen.*

8. R. Arnold Gibbons, "Minority Programming on American Commercial T.V. Network," *Black Academy Review* (Vol. 1, Spring 1970), p. 50.

9. Dr. Joseph Pentecoste, "The New Black Television—A White Strategy: A Commentary," *Inner City Issues,* (Northwestern Illinois State University, October, 1969), p. 11.

10. Unpublished survey by author (Chicago, 1973).

CHAPTER SIX

1. Dista H. Caldwell, *The Education of the Negro Child,* (New York: Carlton Press, 1969), p. 29.

2. Elijah Muhammed, *Message to the Blackman,* (Chicago: Muhammad Mosque of Islam No. 2, 1965), p. 39.

3. Carter G. Woodson, *Miseducation of the Negro.*

4. Paulo Freire, *Pedagogy of the Oppressed,* (New York: Seabury Press, 1973), p. 66.

CHAPTER SEVEN

1. Information Manual for Board of Directors and Committee Members. Welfare Council of Metropolitan Chicago, (Publication No. 5005, May, 1968).

2. Unpublished statement by the Catalyst, a group of black people with skills, who engaged in a number of confrontations with the the Welfare Council over the latter's insensitivity toward the black community.

3. Commission on Youth Welfare (Municipal Code of Chicago 21-65: Passed 9-25-58, p. 8215).

4. Unpublished paper by dissonant members of the Commission on Youth Welfare of Chicago (May 29, 1968).

5. Office of the Mayor, Chicago Model Cities Program, *Year One* (1967), p. 2.

7. Ralph H. Metcalfe, Jr., "Chicago Model Cities and Neocolonialization," *The Black Scholar* (Vol. 1 No. 6, April 1970), p. 24.

8. Ibid., p. 30.

CHAPTER EIGHT

1. Frank Tannenbaum, *Crime and the Community,* (New York: Ginn and Company, 1938), p. 25.

2. Nicholas Alex, *Black In Blue, A Study of the Negro Policeman,* (New York: Appleton-Century-Crofts, 1969), p. 18.

3. Lerone Bennett Jr., *Before the Mayflower,* (Chicago: Johnson Publishing Co., Inc., 1969), p. 75.

4. Francis Ward, "Gloves Davis: A Cop of the Old School," *Chicago Journalism Review,* (Association of Working Press, Inc. Vol. 2, No. 12, Chicago, Ill. 1969), p. 9.

5. Untitled Phamphlet published by the Afro-American Patrolmen's League (Chicago, Ill, 1969).

6. Chicago Police Department Training Division, *Youth-Law-Police,* (Date undisclosed), p. 10.

7. Howard James, *Children In Trouble, A National Scandal,* (New York: David McKay Company, Inc., 1970), p. 75.

8. Unpublished manuscript by Jimmy Jackson (Chicago, 1971).

9. Ibid.

CHAPTER NINE

1. Office of Policy Planning and Research, United States Department of Labor, *The Negro Family, The Case for National Action,* (March, 1965), p. 5.

2. Robert B. Hill, *The Strengths of Black Families,* (New York: Emerson Hall Publishers, Inc., 1971), p. 38.

3. Andrew Billingsley, *Black Families in White America,* (New Jersey: Prentice Hall, Inc., 1968), p. 4.

CHAPTER TEN

1. Dr. Alvin F. Poussaint, "The Negro American: His Self-Image and Integration" (An unpublished paper presented at the 71st Annual Meeting of the National Medical Association, August 8, 1966, in Chicago, Illinois), p. 3.

2. Ibid., p. 2.

3. An unpublished survey made by the author.

4. Eugene Perkins, "The Black Arts Movement: Its Challenge and Responsibility," ed: Floyd B. Barbour (Boston, Mass: Porter Sargent Publisher, 1968), p. 92.

CHAPTER ELEVEN

1. W. E. Burgardt DuBois, *The Gift of Black Folk,* (Boston: The Stratford Co., 1924), p. iii.

CHAPTER TWELVE

1. Kofi Antubam, *Ghana's Heritage of Culture,* (Koehler & Amelang 1963), p. 48.

2. Workshop on the Independent Black Institution, (Palo Alto, Calif, 1970), p. 2.

3. Informational Brochure published by Shule Ya Wote, (Chicago, Ill, 1973), p. 2.

4. Unpublished paper by Paulette Jones (Chicago 1974).

$+16 = 02815$